The School Principal

The School Principal

SAMUEL GOLDMAN

Chairman, Area of Educational Administration,
Supervision and Curriculum
Syracuse University

The Center for Applied Research in Education, Inc.
New York

Library of Congress
Catalog Card No.: 66-15221

PRINTED IN THE UNITED STATES OF AMERICA

Foreword

The principalship in American schools has existed for more than a century. From modest beginnings it has emerged as an extremely important administrative post in education. Its significance is registered not only through numbers—there are more principals than any other educational administrative officer—but also by the strength of the educational programs developed under the leadership of the many outstanding men and women who have held these administrative positions.

Professor Goldman focuses his writing on the evolution of the principalship, the limitations which surround the press for specialization in the principalship by organizational level, and the research completed in recent years with relevance to these offices. Early programs of professional preparation for the principalship highlighted the uniqueness of the position by organizational level. Emphasis on the unique aspects of the principalship at elementary, secondary, and junior high school levels has tended to submerge the commonalities and, to some extent, has mitigated against more rapid perfection of a broader and more useful conception of the principalship.

The author has drawn on wide and diverse literature to gain insight into the role of principalship. As a result, the principalship assumes a new significance in this volume and emerges with an integrity of its own. Research on the principalship has at best been less than what the profession would have willed. At the same time this writing tends to add up to more than most observers would have acknowledged existed. There is evidence that emphasis upon research, and particularly utilization of concepts in professional inquiry from the broader behavioral sciences, is beginning to pay off.

In the past three decades several studies of consequence have gone forward through resources made available primarily by the W. K. Kellogg Foundation and more recently from the U.S. Office of Education. Citations to this research reflect heavily the professional thrust provided by the Cooperative Program in Educational Administration of the early 1950's, and subsequent stimulation

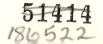

growing out of the University Council for Educational Administration and the professional organizations of principals. The tenor of Professor Goldman's presentation suggests however that considerable work remains to be done. Further emphasis on the behavior of principals vis-a-vis their organizations is in order.

The nature of contemporary affairs is such that each unit of school organization under the direction of a principal must be extraordinarily adaptive to its own milieu. Through the leadership of its principal, each school organization must seek new kinds of data about itself and its performance. These data should include observations about the internal structure and operation of the many social systems which comprise a single unit of school organization, and also the interactions of the school organization with its immediate and extended environments. Increasingly, the principal must become a data specialist; that is, he must come to understand the importance of new kinds of information in administrative decision making. He must come to appreciate the effect of feedback of information about his organization upon its own performance.

An adaptive or an innovative organization is one that capitalizes on feedback and uses feedback data for altering the organization. Leadership in effecting change is, as the author has observed, one of the severest tests facing today's principals. Obviously, much more needs to be known about innovative people and innovative organizations in education. Professor Goldman's work on the principalship dramatizes the magnitude of this task. His book appears at a time when there is a burgeoning interest in change-phenomena. It behooves the educator to keep abreast of the writing on change and innovation and to try as best he can to understand the relevance of such literature to his job, his organization, and his clientele.

LUVERN L. CUNNINGHAM
Director, Midwest Administration Center
Department of Education
University of Chicago

The School Principal

Samuel Goldman

A key administrative position in the public schools is that of principal. As the "man-in-the-middle" posed between central administration and the teaching staff, the principal must put into operation the policies of the school district while, at the same time, he must meet the personal and professional needs of the teachers. While at times these factors may be congruent, at other times they are in conflict. The position of principal incurs other conflicts as well. While the central administration and the teachers hold certain expectations of the principal, community groups may have other views which further complicate the life of the principal. Moreover, the principal's professional organizations may set expectations which are in conflict with all the groups mentioned above. It is into this cauldron that many "mere" men are thrust.

Professor Goldman has handled a difficult assignment well. He has synthesized a rather sizeable body of research. His method of presentation is clear and concise. *The School Principal* is a definite contribution to the literature on school administration.

Dr. Goldman discusses the development of the principalship from the "head teacher" through to the modern day. He carefully integrates present-day research with his theme using, for example, role concepts to set the tone of the basic description. The responsibilities of the principal are discussed in terms of the functions he must perform. Chapters on leader behavior and on leader preparation conclude the book.

Present day and future school principals face challenges on many significant issues—such as integration, church-state relations, teacher militancy, and leadership. The vitality and importance of the role of the principalship as an administrative office will develop only in accordance with the way in which these issues are resolved.

Professor Goldman holds his doctorate from the University of Chicago and is now Chairman, Area of Administration, Supervision, and Curriculum at the School of Education, Syracuse University. He has contributed to research literature and has been very active in the National Conference of Professors of Educational Administration and the University Council for Educational Administration.

DANIEL E. GRIFFITHS
Content Editor

Contents

CHAPTER IX

Preparation for the Principalship 93

CHAPTER I

The Development of the Principalship

The term *school principal,* as it is used today, describes the product of an evolutionary period lasting well over a century. Born in response to the many clerical tasks that became necessary as the educational enterprise expanded, the principalship has developed into an important position of leadership in American education. Indeed, it may well be said that no other position in education save that of the superintendent needs to be more responsive to the ever-growing, constantly-changing demands of a citizenry in need of education.

The contemporary expectation for the school principal is that he be a leader in education, but there is a notable lack of uniformity in the quality of leadership among today's principals. The variations from one school to another are astounding. Some principals exercise energetic, offer bold leadership in adaptively reconstructing their schools' programs to accord with the most current needs and developments. Others, by contrast, suffering from *clerical tasks syndrome,* perform only those functions necessary to maintain existing school structures and programs.

In great part, variations in the quality of principalship are a function of poor selection procedures. Some of those holding principalships are just not suited for the position because of inadequate background, poor training, or inappropriate temperament. The literature on the principalship, however, provides few research-validated guidelines for the selection of potentially successful school principals. A school district, then, is left to do the best it can to find and appoint a capable school principal. The results sometimes are not the best.

The peculiarities unique to a school system also can account for variations in performance among school principals. Poor or indifferent leadership from the superintendent, lack of support from the board of education and the community, and inadequate facilities and poorly trained teachers provide little in the way of useful resources with which the principal may work. Such limitations of the school district severely handicap a principal's potential for leadership. Conversely it may be said that a principal's potential for leadership is greatly enhanced when the superintendent provides dynamic leadership, the board of education and the community are highly supportive, the facilities are modern, and the teachers well trained.

Perhaps one of the most important factors contributing to variations in performance among principals is historical in nature. The position has developed slowly, and until recently little attention was paid to the role principals should play in modern education. A review of the literature on the principalship reveals that in the main the traditional prescriptions for the role of the principal have been derived from three sources:

1. The descriptions of school principals of what they do at the grass-roots level of operation;
2. The pronouncements of authorities who by some form of reasoning arrive at descriptions of what the principal should do;
3. The findings of survey research which, on the basis of opinions and comments collected from principals, teachers, and others provide some sort of taxonomy of the *is* and the *ought-to-be* of the principal's role.

While these sources have yielded some useful information, they are limited in their ability to provide the insights necessary to make the principalship a more vital position in education.

In recent years some rather sophisticated and comprehensive research in educational administration has provided deeper insights into the principalship. It is the purpose of this book to examine this research and to derive from it certain implications for the role of the school principal in modern education.

Historical Development

In order to understand the principalship as it is today, it is important to know how the position evolved. It did not begin as a carefully planned, clearly defined position in education; rather, it emerged in response to a multitude of factors, including increases in school enrollments and numbers of teachers employed, and the proliferation of services provided by the school. As the means for dealing with these factors became more complex and more demanding of time, a distinctive role for the school principal began to emerge.

The major source of information on the historical development of the school principal is provided by Pierce,[1] who examined the published reports of the executive officers of twelve large metropolitan systems. Other than Pierce's work, systematically organized information regarding the development of this position is limited, but much of what has happened to the principalship through the past few decades can be pieced together from the general literature on educational administration.

Early beginnings. The modern public school principalship had its beginning in the early high schools[2] about the middle of the 19th century. Designed to serve a select few, the high schools were closely patterned after their European counterparts, and the secondary school principal performed a multitude of duties. "In addition to teaching and administering his school he often served as town clerk, church chorister, official visitor of the sick, bell ringer of the church, grave digger, and court messenger, and performed other occasional duties."[3] The high school principalship predates the elementary school principalship, but both developed in response to similar influences.[4]

The typical early organization for education was a one-room schoolhouse in which one teacher taught all subjects to students at all levels. As cities grew and school enrollments increased, more teachers were added and schools expanded. With the development of grading practices and departmentalization it became increasingly evident that someone in the school building had to be responsible for its administration.

The position of *principal* (i.e. head) *teacher* was thereupon created. In Cincinnati, a committee especially appointed in 1839 by the Board of Education to study the matter, outlined the responsibilities of the principal teacher as follows:

1. To function as the head of the school charged to his care;
2. To regulate the classes and course of instruction of all the pupils;
3. To discover any defects in the school and apply remedies;
4. To make defects known to the visitor or trustee of the ward or district if he were unable to remedy conditions;
5. To give necessary instruction to his assistants;

functions of head-teacher [handwritten margin note]

---

[1] Paul Revere Pierce, *The Origin and Development of the Public School Principalship* (Chicago: The University of Chicago Press, 1935).

[2] *Ibid.,* p. 1.

[3] Paul B. Jacobson, *et al., The Effective School Principal* (Englewood Cliffs, N.J.: Prentice-Hall, Inc., 1963), p. 491.

[4] Pierce, *op. cit.,* p. 1.

    6. To classify pupils;
    7. To safeguard schoolhouses and furniture;
    8. To keep the school clean;
    9. To instruct assistants;
    10. To refrain from impairing the standing of assistants, especially in the eyes of their pupils;
    11. To require the cooperation of his assistants.[5]

The remaining faculty members, called *assistant teachers*, were instructed to:

    1. Regard the principal teacher as head of the school;
    2. Observe his directions;
    3. Guard his reputation;
    4. Make themselves thoroughly acquainted with the rules and regulations adopted for the government of the schools.[6]

The special committee further pointed out that the qualifications for the position of principal teacher were to include a knowledge of teaching methods, an understanding of children's characteristics and behavior, and a feeling for the common problems of schools.[7] Despite the requirements that he have these qualities, the principal teacher never really exercised them, preferring instead to occupy his time with clerical, routine tasks.

But with the growth and expansion of school programs, and, in particular, with the development of grading practices, the inadequacy of the role played by the principal teacher, soon became evident. He needed time to visit classrooms, to observe teachers and to help those who were inadequately prepared for their responsibilities; but his own teaching duties and his preoccupation with clerical tasks did not permit him enough time to provide this instructional leadership that was becoming so necessary.

Finally, in 1857, to meet the situation the principal teachers in Boston were given some released time from teaching for inspection and examination of primary classes.[8] In 1862, the principal teachers in most of the schools in Chicago were relieved of about half their former teaching time,[9] and in New York City by 1867 no principal teacher had a class or grade "for whose progress and efficiency he was specially responsible."[10]

---

[5] *Ibid.*, p. 12.
[6] *Ibid.*
[7] *Ibid.*
[8] *Ibid.*, p. 15.
[9] *Ibid.*
[10] *Ibid.*, p. 16.

Released time from teaching marked a significant turning point for the principalship. The position now enjoyed a professional status it had never before held. Principals came to enjoy a feeling of security and they began to express a desire for autonomy, particularly through resistance to what they apprehended as unreasonable demands from central office.[11]

More significantly, however, "the freeing of the principal from teaching duties to visit other rooms proved the opening wedge for supervision by the principal."[12] Time was being given to the principal so that he might provide assistance to his teaching staff. In the main, however, few principals were equal to this responsibility. Poor preparation and lack of interest in supervision militated against their carrying out this function. The expectations for the principal changed with his release from teaching duties, but his behavior remained as it had been in the past. Pierce makes this clear:

> The principals were slow individually and as a group to take advantage of the opportunities for professional leadership which were granted them. This tendency was especially marked during the period 1895–1910. The principalship was well established from an administrative point of view, and at that point, principals appeared content to rest. Except for sporadic cases, they did little to study their work, experiment with administrative procedures, or publish articles on local administration and supervision. The large body of them were satisfied to attend to clerical and petty routine, administering their schools on a policy of *laissez faire*. They were generally entrenched behind their tenure rights and they usually hesitated to show vigorous leadership to their teachers who naturally were often as reactionary, professionally, as the principals themselves. They were content to use "rule of thumb" procedures in dealing with supervision of instruction.[13]

The early beginnings of the principalship were quite unimpressive. Concerned with details and routine, content to serve as a transmitter of directives from the superintendent to teachers, afraid to experiment and to innovate, interested in security and self-preservation, the early school principal did little to establish himself as an educational leader. It was not until the 1920's that a serious attempt was made to focus upon the principalship as an important position in education.

1920–30. In 1920, under the guidance of the Department of

---

[11] *Ibid.*, p. 17.
[12] *Ibid.*, p. 16.
[13] *Ibid.*, p. 21.

Education of the University of Chicago, a national organization of elementary school principals was founded. It turned the attention of the principal to scientific study of the problems of his position and stimulated professional interest in the principalship as an important position in American education.[14] The principalship became a topic of study in university departments of education and programs for the training of principals began to appear in the offerings of these departments.

Studies of the principal's job began to appear in professional magazines and journals. In the main these studies were concerned with such factors as the duties and functions of the school principal, the proper use of time in carrying out these functions, and the delegation of administrative functions to assistants.[15] A few representative studies will illustrate this point.

Fillers categorized the managerial duties of the principal as clerical, generalized control, inspectorial, and coordinative. He concluded that many duties could be delegated to teachers and clerks, leaving the principal free to perform duties of more importance to the educational program.[16]

Stanton, on the basis of a time study of office routines, proposed several time-saving administrative procedures for the principal.[17] Ayers made a study of the value preferences assigned by principals and superintendents to various administrative duties. He concluded:

> A very considerable individual variation in the selection of duties might well be expected, but the general lack of balance in the selection of duties and the emphasis placed upon duties of minor value by many administrators has impressed the author as being due either to lack of foresight in planning, or to a lack of knowledge as to what constitutes a proper program of administrative duties.[18]

Ayers's observations emphasized the need for school administrators to acquire a better understanding of administrative procedure. After 1930, studies focusing on this need were pursued with vigor,

---

[14] *Ibid.,* p. 22.

[15] For a comprehensive analysis of the attempt to use scientific management in education during this period, see Raymond E. Callahan, *Education and the Cult of Efficiency* (Chicago: The University of Chicago Press, 1962).

[16] Harold D. Fillers, "The Managerial Duties of the Principal," *School Review,* XXVIII (January 1923), 48–53.

[17] Edgard A. Stanton, "Saving Time in Office Routine," *Elementary School Journal,* XXVII (December 1927), 263–272.

[18] Fred C. Ayers, "The Duties of Public School Administrators," *American School Board Journal,* LXXXX (May 1930), 44.

and the findings assumed an important place in the literature on the principalship.

At the university level, programs for the training of school administrators reflected the prevailing managerial orientation to school administration. These programs stressed the practical skills necessary to acquire and keep an administrative job in education.

> The result was an emphasis upon the techniques and the mechanics of administration. While this kind of program did not require extensive study in the disciplines upon which a real understanding of education must be based and was not oriented toward basic inquiry and the production of knowledge, it did provide students with the knowledge and skills necessary to operate the schools in a business like way—a prerequisite for job survival in most school districts in the twenties.[19]

The school principal was emerging as a technician in education. The central focus of his training was upon such matters as budgeting, school construction, and pupil-accounting. He was beginning to view himself as a business-executive-in-education. The temper of society during this period reinforced that image and even demanded that he hold it.[20]

Since 1930. The 1930's marked the beginning of a series of dramatic events which have had dramatic implications for mankind generally and for education specifically. Starting with the economic depression of the 1930's, the face of education began to take on a new look, and a new philosophy of educational administration slowly took shape.

This philosophy did not come from within education itself. It came, rather, from the work of industrial psychologists, sociologists, and others interested in the study of organizations and the people who worked in them. Among the major contributors were: Mary Parker Follett,[21] who brought into sharper focus the psychological

---

19 Raymond E. Callahan and H. Warren Button, "Historical Change of Role of the Man in the Organization: 1865–1950," in *Behavioral Science and Educational Administration,* Sixty-Third Yearbook of the National Society for the Study of Education, Part II, edited by Daniel E. Griffiths (Chicago: University of Chicago Press, 1964) pp. 88–89.

20 For a discussion of the response of school administration to the social pressures of this time see Raymond E. Callahan, *Education and the Cult of Efficiency, op. cit.,* especially pp. 179–220.

21 For example, see H. C. Metcalf and L. Urwick, eds., *Dynamic Administration: The Collected Papers of Mary Parker Follett* (New York: Harper & Bros., 1940).

aspects of administration; Mayo,[22] Roethlisberger,[23] and others who underscored the importance of human relations in administration; Barnard[24] who in *The Functions of the Executive* explored with deep insight the theory of organization and laid the groundwork for further theorizing on the role of the executive; and finally Simon,[25] who worked to develop a useful value-free science of administration. These writers and others made substantial contributions to the emerging body of knowledge in educational administration.[26]

The move to apply this knowledge in educational administration was slow[27] and it was not until 1950 that the study of educational administration took a turn[28] which provided many important implications for the principalship. Major emphasis was directed away from analyses of functions and duties and towards analysis of superior-subordinate relationships within the school setting.

Theories of leadership, society, interpersonal relationships, and administrative behavior drawn from the academic disciplines have increasingly become important elements in the study of educational administration. Specifically, the works of Mort, Sears, and Getzels have pulled together important concepts from these disciplines, and have paved the way to new understandings in educational administration.[29]

Despite developments in the philosophy of educational administration generally, the body of knowledge specifically for the principalship has not kept pace. At least three obstacles hinder a clear understanding of the principalship.

---

[22] Elton Mayo, *The Human Problems of an Industrial Civilization* (Cambridge: Harvard University Press, 1933); *The Social Problems of an Industrial Civilization* (Cambridge: Harvard University Press, 1945).

[23] Fritz Roethlisberger, *Management and Morale* (Cambridge: Harvard University Press, 1941).

[24] Chester Barnard, *The Functions of the Executive* (Cambridge: Harvard University Press, 1938).

[25] Herbert A. Simon, *Administrative Behavior* (New York: The MacMillan Company, 1957).

[26] For a more extensive discussion of the contributions of the writers mentioned here see Bertram Gross, "The Scientific Approach to Administration," in *Behavioral Science and Educational Administration, op. cit.,* pp 33–72.

[27] For a brief discussion on this move see Raymond E. Callahan and H. Warren Button, *op. cit., loc. cit.,* pp. 89–92.

[28] For a discussion of this see Hollis A. Moore, Jr., "The Ferment in School Administration," in *Behavioral Science and Educational Administration, op. cit.,* pp. 11–32.

[29] For a discussion of the contributions of these writers and others see Daniel E. Griffiths, "Some Attempts at Theorizing in Administration," in *Administrative Theory* (New York: Appleton-Century-Crofts, Inc., 1959), pp. 47–70.

Obstacles to Understanding the Principalship

A clear view of the principalship has been impeded by several factors, but chiefly by the following three:

1. Insularity of principalships;
2. Local school district uniquenesses;
3. Imprecise definition of the role.

Insularity of principalships. Historically, three variant principalship positions have emerged; in order of appearance, the high school principalship, the elementary school principalship and the junior high school principalship. Each of the first two positions has its own identity, professional association, and bulletin.[30] But the junior high school principalship, still lacking a clear identity of its own, tends to identify with the high school principalship, the two undifferentiated positions sometimes being referred to collectively as the *secondary school principalship.*[31]

This specialization by level has led to equally specialized bodies of literature, each relying heavily on contributions from authors whose interests lie in the same place. Training programs and certification requirements for school principals have also tended to foster the trend to specialization. Students can study to become specifically elementary school principals, or secondary school principals. Training programs for the several levels tend to overlap in certain areas, but the central aim is nevertheless to train people for a specific level of the principalship.

This insularity has led to several rather narrow and constricting milieus within which school principals tend to move. The principals at each level hold common professional cause with their fellow principals in the same level, at the cost, often, of communication with principals at the other levels. The emphasis on differences among the various principalship levels that may be more apparent than real makes it difficult to focus on the principalship as a singular entity.

Local school district uniquenesses. A lack of uniformity among school districts with regard to grade organization further clouds the

---

[30] See *The Bulletin of the National Association of Secondary School Principals* (Washington, D.C.: The Association, National Education Association); *The National Elementary Principal* (Washington, D.C.: Department of Elementary School Principals, National Education Association).

[31] See *The Bulletin of the National Association of Secondary School Principals, The Junior High School: Position Papers and Practices* (Washington, D.C.: The Association, Vol. 47, No. 285, October 1963).

view of the principalship. For example, a school district may organize in any one of a number of grade patterns: 6–3–3; 6–2–4; 6–6; 4–4–4; or 5–4–3. Thus a senior high school principal may be responsible for three grades in one district (grades 10 through 12); four grades in another district (grades 9 through 12); or six grades in yet another district (grades 6 through 12). These varying patterns imply differing responsibilities for the elementary and junior high school principal as well.

There are other factors deriving from the local district's organization that influence the expectations for the principal's job. His tasks at any level may be determined in large measure by one or a combination of the following factors:

1. Size of the school district;
2. Size of the school staff;
3. Number of administrative assistants in the school building; (e.g. assistant principals, department chairmen, area coordinators and the like);
4. Scope of the educational program;
5. Nature of the district-wide administrative organization;
6. Varied expectations by professional and lay publics for his job performance;
7. Financial ability of the school district.

It may well be that little can be done to remove the district-organization obstacle to viewing the principalship. School districts will continue to differ from one another making it very difficult to establish a universally acceptable set of expectations for the principalship.

Imprecise definition of the role. The differentiation of the principalship into several job levels has tended to obfuscate rather than define the role, and the fact that no two school districts seem to have quite the same expectations for one and the same job level further muddles the situation. There is need for intensive study of the principalship, using a generic rather than specific approach, to systematize and explain the common phenomena underlying all levels of this position. These phenomena could then form the base upon which a more precise definition for the role of the school principal can be developed.

There is evidence which suggests that there are certain areas of commonality between the principalship and other positions in educational administration. In a review of the literature on competencies needed by school superintendents, principals, and supervisors, Woodward found that out of 203 identifiable competencies 70 per cent were common to all three positions, 84 per cent of those listed as essential for the principal were also listed as essential for the superintendent, and 92 per cent of the competencies listed as essential for the principal were also listed as essential for the supervisor.[32] These commonalities suggest that there can be similarity in ways of viewing the principalship and other positions in educational administration.

Ways of Viewing the Principalship

In the past fifteen years there have emerged some fruitful concepts by which the role of the school administrator may be viewed. The so-called Tri-Dimensional Concept,[33] for example, originally developed to describe the role of the superintendent, provides a model by which all administrative positions in education including the principalship may be understood. The model posits a definite relationship among three dimensions—the administrator's job, the type of person he is, and the milieu within which he carries out his responsibilities.

Another useful approach to understanding the role of the administrator is advanced by Katz, who suggests that to be effective an administrator must employ what Katz describes as *technical, human,* and *conceptual* skills, which he defines as follows:

Technical Skill . . . An understanding of, and proficiency in, a specific kind of activity, particularly one involving methods, processes, procedures or techniques. Technical skill involves specialized knowledge, analytical ability within that specialty, and facility in the use of the tools and techniques of the specific discipline.
Human Skill . . . The executive's ability to work effectively as a group member and to build cooperative effort within the team he leads.
Conceptual Skill . . . The ability to see the enterprise as a whole; it includes recognizing how the various functions of the organization depend on one another, and how changes in any one part affect all the others. Recognizing those relationships and perceiving the sig-

---

[32] Pierce B. Woodward, "A Study of Competencies Needed by School Administrators and Supervisors in Virginia with Implications for Pre-Service Education" (Doctoral dissertation, CPEA Project. Charlotte, Va.: University of Virginia, 1953) reported in Edgar L. Morphet, R. L. Johns, and Theodore L. Reller, *Educational Administration: Concepts, Practices and Issues* (Englewood Cliffs, N.J.: Prentice-Hall, Inc., 1959) pp. 283–284.
[33] *A Developing Concept of the Superintendency of Education,* rev. ed. (Albany, N.Y.: Cooperative Development of Public School Administration, 1955).

nificant elements in any situation, the administrator should then be able to act in a way which advances the over-all welfare of the total organization.[34]

This book will not focus upon any specific formulation of the principalship. Rather, it will attempt to survey many of the relevant formulations, in the course of which it will describe the role played by the principal as he relates to his many reference groups; the major functions of this position; the research and literature on the leadership behavior of school principals; and the preparation needed for entering the principalship.

The state of knowledge regarding the principalship is still quite young. For this reason there are many gaps in what is known of the principalship. The reader will become aware of this as he sees the style of this book change from a reporting of research data with implications for the principalship to a collection of statements supported by little or no research, but which, through inference, describe what the principal *should* do in certain circumstances. There is much research that needs yet to be done to fill in these gaps.

---

[34] Robert L. Katz, "Skills of an Effective Administrator," *Harvard Business Review,* Vol. 33, No. 1 (January-February 1955), 34–42.

CHAPTER II

The Role of the School Principal

In recent years there has been a pronounced shift in the orientation of studies of educational administration, away from "What does the school administrator do?" toward "What is his role in the total educational enterprise?" The latter path of inquiry has led to some interesting and important research on the administrator's relationship to his reference groups, the decision-making process, and the potential for conflict in the educational organization.

The Definition of Role

Starting with Linton's view that roles are the dynamic aspects of the positions, offices, and statuses within an institution,[1] Getzels has postulated that roles have "certain obligations and responsibilities, which may be termed *role expectations,* and when the role incumbent puts these obligations and responsibilities into effect he is said to be *performing his role.*"[2]

The role of the school principal carries with it certain expectations for behavior and for performance that derive from many sources; notably, from what are known as the principal's *reference groups.* When the principal acts and performs in an expected manner he is conforming to the role expectations held for him by his reference groups.

Why must the principal conform with the expectations of others? The answer to this question is not easy, for at first glance it appears as if the principal is operating as an other-directed administrator. In part this is correct, for there are individuals and groups both within and outside the school system who hold certain expectations for the principal's role and who assess his effectiveness in terms of the extent to which he meets these expectations. The rationale of the principal's attunement to the expectation of others may be found

---

[1] Ralph Linton, *The Study of Man* (New York: Appleton-Century-Crofts, Inc., 1936), p. 14.
[2] Jacob W. Getzels, "Administration as a Social Process," in *Administrative Theory in Education,* Andrew W. Halpin, ed. (Chicago: Midwest Administration Center, The University of Chicago, 1958), p. 153.

in the very nature of the control of the schools. The principal must be sensitive to the educational expectations of others and, where possible, he must attempt to meet them. He is not at liberty to conduct the affairs of the school solely on the basis of his own expectations.

This rationale suggests the second and perhaps most important reason for considering and, where possible, for meeting the expectations of others. There are many in the school system who play roles complementary to that of the principal. These include teachers, supervisors, and the like. The principal cannot perform his own role without giving some consideration to how his performance might affect or infringe upon the roles of others. In essence, then, these others, called *referents* of the principal, play an important part in the definition and delineation of his role.

Functionally, the role of the principal can best be understood in terms of his relationship to and involvement with his intraorganizational and extraorganizational referents. An *intraorganizational referent* is one who is employed by the school district as, say, a teacher, administrator, or custodian, or who is a direct recipient of its services, a student. An *extraorganizational referent* is one who is not employed by the district but who is an indirect recipient of its services, as, say, a parent, or one who is indirectly involved with the operations of the school, a taxpayer.[3]

The Intraorganizational Role

His intraorganizational role calls for the principal to bring together materials, resource persons, teachers, and pupils in a positive relationship so as to effect intellectual development and social growth in the learners. This is a role common to principals at all levels, and principals should be devoting a major portion of their time directly to providing conditions for and stimulating activities designed to enhance the processes of teaching and learning.

This role relates the principal structurally and functionally to many other positions within the school districts. Figures 2–1 and 2–2 depict two such formal structures.

---

[3] An important referent omitted in this discussion is the profession itself. The principal plays a role within a total profession and is therefore subject to some influences from colleagues in his profession. However, because his colleagues within the context of the profession are not crucially related to the role played by the principal in his own school district, they will not be discussed here. Some reference will be made to the importance of the profession in the concluding chapter.

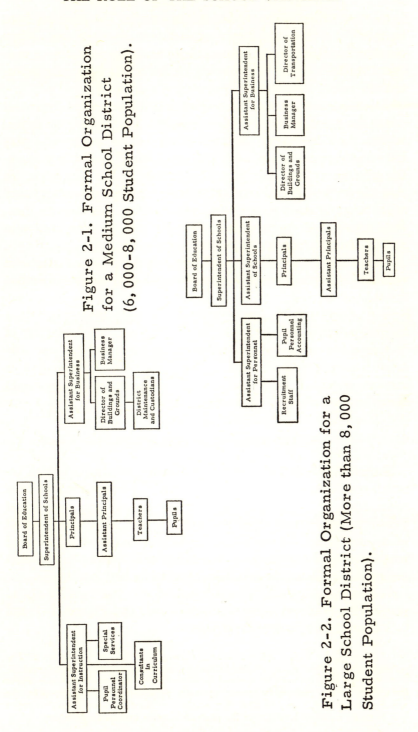

Figure 2-1. Formal Organization for a Medium School District (6,000-8,000 Student Population).

Figure 2-2. Formal Organization for a Large School District (More than 8,000 Student Population).

In Fig. 2–1 the principal is shown in a line relationship, reporting directly to the superintendent of schools. This enables him to interact directly with the chief school administrator and thus to influence school policies. In school systems organized this way the superintendent meets regularly with an administrative council composed of all the principals in the school district. (See p. 15.)

Figure 2–2 depicts an organization necessitated by large school systems, in which the principal is removed one line-step away from the chief school administrator. In this organization the Assistant Superintendent of Schools is the immediate superior referent of the school principal. (See p. 15.)

In both organizational schema the school principal occupies a man-in-the-middle position between the chief school administrator or his immediate assistant and the teachers. By virtue of his designation as head of the instructional unit, the principal occupies a superior position in relation to his staff, but on the other hand, he is subordinate to the chief school administrator. The result is that the school principal has referents from above, his superiors, and from below, his subordinates.

This situation poses somewhat of a dilemma for him. It often happens that the expectations from the principal's various referents are divergent, even conflicting. In a study of the leadership behavior of high school principals, Evenson found marked disparities among the expectations of teachers, superintendents, and principals for the principal's leadership behavior.[4] Sometimes the differences are easily resolved; in certain cases the referents are content to live with them. However, disparate expectations for such substantive areas as grading practices, content of instruction, and the like could lead to considerable conflict and tension. In such cases, the principal must resolve the disparities without dividing the groups and with no harm to any party. How he resolves the differences among his referents will be influenced by (1) his own values, beliefs and needs; (2) the depth of his insight into significant problems and issues; (3) his own perceptions of his role; (4) his vulnerability to pressures and influences; and (5) his ability to lead.

The principal and his superior.   In many ways the principal

---

[4] Warren L. Evenson, "The Leadership Behavior of High School Principals: Perceptions and Expectations of Superintendents, Principals, and Staff Members" (unpublished Doctoral dissertation, Dept. of Education, University of Chicago, 1958). See Chapter 8 of this book for a report of Evenson's findings.

of a school and the superintendent of a school system hold somewhat complementary positions in the administration of the educational program. The board of education, working with and through the superintendent, its chief executive officer and professional advisor, outlines the parameters of policy that will govern the school system. The superintendent provides the leadership and the support for developing the program for the system as a whole, and the principal assumes the responsibility for carrying it out at the local level. In effect, the principal and staff of each school are expected to develop and to provide an educational program therein which is within the policy framework established by the board of education and the superintendent.

The superintendent is an important referent to the school principal. How much he influences the behavior of the school principal is related to the directness of the linkage between the two of them. Gross and Herriott made a study of characteristics descriptive of what they termed the *Executive Performance Leadership of elementary school principals.*[5] They found that in school systems where the superintendent was not the immediate superior to the elementary school principal, "the professional leadership of superintendents and the administrative and social support they gave principals are not related to Executive Performance Leadership."[6] Gross and Herriott provide evidence to indicate that the principal's immediate superior, whatever position he holds, is regarded as a major referent for the principal's role. They found, for example, that:

1. There is a positive relationship between the professional leadership of a principal's immediate administrative superior and the principal's own Executive Performance Leadership.[7]
2. The administrative support displayed by the principal's immediate administrative superior does not play the same part in influencing the principal's Executive Performance Leadership as does the former's professional leadership.[8]
3. The Executive Performance Leadership of elementary school prin-

---

[5] Neal Gross and Robert E. Herriott, *The Professional Leadership of Elementary School Principals* (Washington, D.C.: Cooperative Research Branch, Project No. 853, U.S. Office of Education, April 1964). *Executive Performance Leadership* (EPL) is defined as "the behavior of executives of professionally staffed organizations that reflect efforts to facilitate the achievement of organizational objectives through influencing staff members" (Chapter 1, p. 11).

[6] *Ibid.*, Chaper 6, p. 14.

[7] *Ibid.*, p. 4.

[8] *Ibid.*, p. 8.

cipals, in part, is affected by the social support that they receive from their immediate superiors.[9]

These data suggest that his immediate superior exerts the greatest influence on the administrative performance of the school principal. It appears then, that a referent important for definition of the principal's role is the administrator to whom the principal is directly responsible.

The principal and central office personnel.   Another important referent for the principal's intraorganizational role is the staff of the central office. This includes all those positions which attach to the superintendent's office and which operate on a system-wide rather than intraschool level, including subject matter and general coordinators, consultants or supervisors, assistant school superintendents, and the like. Such positions are in a staff rather than line relationship to the school principal.[10] There is little research which deals directly with the role relationship between the school principal and the central office staff, but it is clear there are certain relationships which contribute to effective performance of both roles.[11]

Personnel from the central office are important to the principal in many ways. To supplement his own efforts to help his teachers, the principal may call upon certain of the supervisors or resource people from the central office to assist in program development or to aid in fostering the professional growth of the teachers. In cooperation with the principal, these specialists usually establish an ongoing program of classroom visitation for purposes of aiding teachers in program development and execution.

In most cases, members of the central office staff hold no administrative power or authority over the principal. The role of the specialist is that of consultant only, he is not a competitor for the allegiance of teachers. Typically, central office personnel work with the school staff through the principal.

The principal and his assistants.   In a study to determine criteria of successful performance for elementary school principals, it

---

[9] *Ibid.*, p. 12. Social support refers to the behavior of the superior which is measured by the following items: integrity in behavior, interest in personal welfare, developing a *we*-feeling in working with others, rubbing people the wrong way, making those who work with him feel inferior to him, his ability to put you at ease when you talk with him.

[10] For a discussion of organizational structure, see Daniel E. Griffiths, *et al.*, *Organizing Schools for Effective Education* (Danville, Ill.: Interstate Publishers Inc., 1962).

[11] For a comprehensive discussion of the role of central office personnel, see Edwin A. Fensch and Robert E. Wilson, *The Superintendency Team* (Columbus, Ohio: Charles E. Merrill Books Inc., 1964).

was found that there was very little delegation in the simulated elementary school which was used in the project.[12] The researchers suggest that this finding is reasonable in that there usually is no one in the elementary school to whom certain responsibilities could realistically be assigned. They conclude that "Delegation should not be expected in elementary schools until the schools are staffed with personnel to whom principals can delegate."[13]

Assistant principals may be found in some large elementary schools performing duties assigned to them by the principal. Depending upon the administrative structure established by the principal, his assistant may or may not be in a line relationship to the teachers. Where he is not in a line position, the assistant principal holds no formal authority over the teachers in the building.

As elementary school programs increase in size and scope, the need for assistants to the principal will increase. Studies need to be made of the role the assistant principal might play, his relationship to others in the school, and the responsibilities that might be vested in the position. Changes in the assistant principal's role will affect the role of the principal, too. This relationship needs careful study.

Assistants to the principal are more prevalent at the high school level because of the departmentalized nature of the program. Department chairmen, deans of boys and girls, guidance coordinators, assistant principals, and others directly aid the principal in the administration of the school. At this level of organization teachers are often directly responsible to an administrator who is subordinate to the principal; for example, teachers in a given department will be directly responsible to the department chairman. Studies of the ramifications of this type of organization need to be made.

The principal and noncertificated personnel. The category of noncertificated personnel includes mainly clerks and custodians. Clerks handle routine matters of noninstructional nature. In most elementary schools the principal has at least one secretary who handles telephone calls, correspondence, filing, requisition and distribution of supplies, and the like. In the secondary schools there may be several clerks, each perhaps handling some specific matter such as pupil attendance, record-keeping, bookkeeping, secretarial tasks, or the like.

---

[12] The study is reported in John K. Hemphill, Daniel E. Griffiths, and Norman Frederiksen, *Administrative Performance and Personality* (New York: Bureau of Publications, Teachers College, Columbia University, 1962).

[13] *Ibid.,* p. 347.

The maintenance of school equipment and property is carried on by the custodial staff. The custodial staff, often including women as well as men, has the responsibility of keeping plant equipment in good working condition, cleaning the school building, maintaining the grounds around the building, moving furniture to desired locations within the building, and so on. The pattern of administering custodial services varies greatly among school districts. In many districts, custodians are responsible to a central office director of buildings and grounds; in other districts, custodial services are contractually supplied by a commercial agency to whom the custodians are responsible. However, while he is working in a particular school building, a custodian should be directly responsible to the principal of that building for the day-to-day maintenance of the plant and the grounds.

There has been no rigorous research which describes the relationship between the principal and clerks and custodians. But because the principal is the designated head of the unit within which both clerks and custodians work, it is incumbent upon him to supervise them. The principal must seek to identify the professional and personal needs of the noncertificated personnel in his jurisdiction and to work with them so that achievements are mutually satisfying.

The principal and his teachers.   Probably no other referent group is more important to the school principal than the group of teachers who work in his building. In describing the role relationship between a teacher and his principal, Guba and Bidwell make this comment:

> Thus, within a school, teacher and principal are in a complementary role relationship. Each holds role expectations which serve to define the behavior of the other; each perceives and evaluates the behavior of the other; and each sanctions, positively or negatively, the observed behavior of the other. Hence, for the role of the teacher the principal is a legitimate *alter* and vice versa. At the same time each incumbent brings to the role his unique personality structure which, in interaction with the role expectations of the relevant alters, results in obversed role behavior.[14]

In a study of teachers and principals in eight secondary and sixteen elementary schools, Guba and Bidwell sought to determine the relationships between role expectations, teacher effectiveness, job

---

[14] Egon G. Guba and Charles E. Bidwell, *Administrative Relationships* (Chicago: The Midwest Administration Center, University of Chicago, 1957), p. 1.

satisfaction, and confidence in leadership of the principal.[15] Their findings may be summarized as follows:

1. Whatever the reality of the situation may be, the ratings of effectiveness which a principal gives to a teacher are a function of the degree to which he perceives that the teacher is conforming to the expectations which he holds for the teacher role.

2. Also independent of the nature of the "real" organizational world, a teacher's self-rating of effectiveness is a function of his perceptions of the principal's expectations as compared with his self-perceptions of job performance.

3. The satisfaction which a teacher expresses in his job is a function of the extent to which the instructional expectations perceived by the teacher are congruent with the expectations which the teacher feels ought to be held for him (idealized expectations.)

4. The confidence in the principal's leadership which is exhibited by a teacher is a function of the congruence between the teacher's perception of administrative expectations and the teacher's idealized version of those expectations.

5. All aspects of staff relations dealt with in this study—satisfaction, confidence in leadership, and effectiveness on the job—seem closely related to the extent to which the perceptions, both of expectations and of behavior, held by principals and by teachers coincide.[16]

Other studies on principal-teacher relationships have substantiated and expanded the work of Guba and Bidwell. Moyer, for example, in a study of teacher attitudes and expectations of leadership, found that:

> Teachers have a mental picture of an "ideal leader" with whom they would like to work in their school situation, and as their leader-ideal picture more nearly coincides with the type of leadership they perceive to exist in the situation, their feelings of satisfaction from working in the school are increased.[17]

Bidwell found that teachers' views of their principals were determined largely by the degree to which the principals conformed to the teachers' expectations. He found that "dissatisfied teachers said that they could not predict how their administrators would act, while satisfied teachers could easily predict how their administrators would act and what would be expected of them as teachers."[18] Bidwell further pointed out that the feeling of security which came from

---

[15] *Ibid.*

[16] *Ibid.*, pp. 65–68.

[17] Donald C. Moyer, "Leadership that Teachers Want," *Administrator's Notebook,* Vol. 3, No. 7 (March 1955).

[18] Charles E. Bidwell, "Some Causes of Conflict and Tension Among Teachers," *Administrator's Notebook,* Vol. 4, No. 7 (March 1956).

the knowledge that they occupied a definite and secure professional role in the school system often was generalized by the teachers into a feeling of satisfaction with the operation of the entire school system.[19]

The personal needs and desires of teachers are also important factors in the teacher-principal relationship. Campbell found this in a study of eight elementary and seven secondary schools:[20]

1. Teachers whose wants and needs were in agreement with their principal's expectations expressed significantly higher job satisfaction than those whose wants were in conflict with the principal's definition of the teacher's role.

2. Teachers whose wants and needs were in agreement with what the principal expected expressed more confidence in leadership than did teachers whose wants were in conflict with the principal's expectations.[21]

Andrews, in a study of 564 teachers and principals including nearly the total faculties of eight large high schools, found that high school teachers differ in psychological characteristics according to their subject matter fields.[22] He concluded from this that:

If teachers differ in personality needs, dominant values, and educational attitudes according to their subject matter fields, then sectionalism and conflict of interest between groups in a high school is a potential danger.[23]

The important implication of this finding is that the principal must work to keep teachers' perceptions of their role in proper perspective, thus to avert schism among the school staff. Equally important is the need for the principal to clearly establish his own role as leader of the group and coordinator of group activity. In this way he can foster group cohesion by keeping in proper focus the mutual goals toward which the entire professional staff is striving.

Based upon the research reported thus far, the following conclusions on teacher-principal role relations seem warranted:

1. The perceived effectiveness of the principal by the teacher, and the perceived effectiveness of the teacher by the principal are dependent upon each fulfilling the role expectations held by the other.

---

[19] *Ibid.*
[20] Merton V. Campbell "Teacher-Principal Agreement on the Teacher Role," *Administrator's Notebook,* Vol. 7, No. 6 (February 1959).
[21] *Ibid.*
[22] John M. Andrews "A Deterrent to Harmony Among Teachers," *Administrator's Notebook,* Vol. 6, No. 7 (March 1958).
[23] *Ibid.*

2. Each role incumbent, principal and teacher, brings with him a unique personality structure which, in interaction with others, guides personal behavior.

3. Teachers have an "ideal image" of the type of principal for whom they would like to work. The more closely a principal approaches that ideal, the greater the job satisfaction experienced by the teachers. Teachers evaluate their principal in accordance with how well he measures up to their conceptualization of an ideal principal.

4. Teachers express greater job satisfaction when they are able to predict the behavior of their principals.

5. Principals rate as most effective those teachers who conform to the role they expect teachers to fulfill.

6. Teachers whose wants and needs are in agreement with what the principal expects express greater confidence in the principal's leadership.

7. Teacher groups which cluster around subject matter fields in a high school exist and can be sources of conflict for the principal.

The implications of these conclusions for the role of the principal as he relates to his teachers are:

1. The principal must clearly communicate to his teachers the role he will play in the school;

2. The principal must clearly communicate to his teachers what he expects of them;

3. The principal's behavior should be consistent as he carries out his role.

The principal and the student. The major school responsibilities for fostering the intellectual and social growth of students are assigned to the teachers and program specialists, leaving the principal's relationship to the student, in normal circumstances, an indirect one. Generally, when the relationship is more direct—as for example in a discipline case—others, such as teachers, program specialists, psychologists and the like, are also usually involved.

In this area, the major role for the school principal is that of pupil personnel administrator. As one observer has defined the role:

> It is concerned with those administrative and supervisory activities and services other than classroom instruction which have as their focus the identification and enrollment of individuals who would benefit from educational experiences, as well as comprehending and developing the abilities, interests, and needs of individuals of varying maturity levels within the school system.[24]

Of primary concern here are those administrative practices related to the identification of pupils through the census, admission pol-

---

[24] Stephen J. Knezevich, *Administration of Public Education* (New York: Harper & Brothers, 1962), p. 328.

icies, enrollment procedures, attendance keeping and classification.[25] Such activities seem rather routine and managerial in nature. It would be wrong to leave the impression that this is the only role the principal plays relative to students. The principal makes his most important contribution to the student through the leadership he provides to teachers and program specialists in developing and implementing curricula which meet the needs of each student enrolled in the school program.

The Extraorganizational Role

Historically and by design, the public schools in the United States belong to the American people. Through their elected representatives on boards of education and by reason of their financial support of the schools, the people in large measure influence the design and content of educational programs. To a great extent this state of affairs contributes to the differences which exist between schools. The unique needs of a community, caused by political forces, geographical location, cultural heritage, social structure, and economic conditions have created vast differences between the school districts in the country and have even created differences between schools within the same district.

The instructional unit—i.e., the school of which the principal is the designated head—may be viewed as the educational center of a unique constellation of community needs. Citizens who live within a particular attendance area form a community of interests not apt to be quite like any other attendance area communities within the same school district.[26] In order that his school's program will reflect the interests of the community it serves and at the same time will be an instrument of desired social change, the principal must be a paramount communicator of purpose both to parents and other citizens (his *extraorganizational reference groups*) and to his professional staff (his *intraorganizational reference groups*).

Community groups. In most communities there are at least four groups that have appreciable influence on school matters:

---

[25] *Ibid.,* p. 329. More discussion on this topic will be found in Chapter VII of this book.

[26] A great deal of emphasis is being given to open enrollment policies which under certain conditions, permit parents to send their children to a school of their choosing. Under such a policy the community served by the school is broadened considerably, providing a more diffuse group for whom an educational program must be provided.

1. The group that takes the leadership in active support for the schools;
2. The group that wants to change things;
3. The group that opposes the school because of a belief that what the school teaches conflicts with certain values which are held;
4. The group that is apathetic and non-vocal, which often lends its support where the pressure is greatest.[27]

Specifically, these groups include PTA's, civic organizations, labor unions, and the like.[28]

Each of these groups has its own peculiar set of needs, desires, expectations, and aspirations, which are expressed as opinions on what functions a school should or should not perform. Downey, for example, in a summary of three companion studies on the task of public education, stated that while there was a high degree of agreement regarding the task of the public school, there were subtle disagreements on the amount of emphasis people were willing to place on certain aspects of these tasks.[29]

Other studies of community groups in education have revealed data which are of importance to the school principal; a few of them will be reported here.

Using a sample of 301 PTA members, Sutthoff was able to identify two types of participant-orientations among citizens active in school affairs.[30] He classed his subjects as *locals* or *cosmopolitans*, depending upon the perspective from which they viewed and participated in school activities. Those having a provincial, community-oriented outlook on school matters he called locals; he described as cosmopolitans those he found to have less affinity with the community than with the world outside it.

Hills examined the views on education held by several social classes, particularly the differing emphases they placed on curriculum orientations; he also studied their preferences of teaching style.[31] Among other things he found that:

1. There were no major differences among social class groups re-

---

[27] Roald F. Campbell and John A. Ramseyer, *The Dynamics of School-Community Relationships* (Boston: Allyn and Bacon Inc., 1958), pp. 19–21.

[28] For a discussion of groups which influence education in a school district, see Neal Gross, *Who Runs Our Schools?* (New York: John Wiley & Sons, 1958).

[29] Lawrence W. Downey, *The Task of Public Education* (Chicago: Midwest Administration Center, The University of Chicago, 1960), p. 64.

[30] John Sutthoff "Local Cosmopolitan Orientation and Participation in School Affairs," *Administrator's Notebook*, Vol. 9, No. 3 (November 1960).

[31] R. Jean Hills, "The Relationship between the Educational Expectations of Social Class Groups and the Role Expectations within the Public High School" (Doctoral dissertation, Department of Education, University of Chicago, 1961).

garding preferred teaching style, with greatest preferenc shown for the nomothetic style of teaching.[32]

2. There were differences among the social classes studied with respect to curriculum orientation expectations. The upper, upper-middle, and middle class respondents indicated a strong preference for an intellectually oriented curriculum. Lower-middle class respondents gave almost equal weight to intellectual, social and vocational orientations. Lower class respondents placed greatest stress on social orientations, followed by vocational and then intellectual. Upper and upper-middle class respondents relegated the vocational aspects of the curriculum to a position of relative unimportance.

3. The teachers from the upper income residential school district reported considerable pressure by parents on the school with the stress upon the value of education achieving and maintaining social status. The teachers from the lower-income semi-industrial suburb reported almost complete freedom from community pressures.[33]

In a study to determine the relationship between attitudes concerning education and attitudes concerning government and society, Levine discerned liberal and conservative viewpoints whose advocates were sources of public school criticism.[34] He states that:

> The charge that the public schools seriously neglect academic objectives receives strongest support from economic conservatives. The charge that the public schools neglect patriotic and "moral" objectives by failing to vigorously affirm traditional values receives strongest support from school conservatives.[35]

McPhee completed a study in which he sought to establish the relationship between individual values, educational viewpoint, and readiness to approve of the local school.[36] Two of his findings are relevant here:

1. Respondents who were emergent in their differential values tended also to be modern in their general educational viewpoint.

2. Respondents with modern educational viewpoints were slightly

---

[32] The nomothetic teaching style places greatest stress upon the obligation of students to adhere to rules and regulations.

[33] R. Jean Hills, "Social Classes and Educational Views," *Administrator's Notebook,* Vol. 10, No. 2 (October 1961).

[34] Daniel U. Levine, "The Relation Between Attitudes Concerning Education and Attitudes Concerning Government and Society" (Doctoral dissertation, Department of Education, University of Chicago, 1963).

[35] Daniel U. Levine, "Liberalism, Conservatism and Educational Viewpoint," *Administrator's Notebook,* Vol. 11, No. 9 (May 1963).

[36] Roderick F. McPhee, "The Relationship Between Individual Values, Educational Viewpoint, and Local School Approval" (Doctoral dissertation, Department of Education, University of Chicago, 1959).

higher in approval of the local schools than those with traditional educational viewpoints.[37]

DeGood, in a study done in Ohio, found that "a superintendent can hold views about education that are contradictory to those held in his community and still be adjudged effective."[38] His data led him to conclude that the capacity to accurately perceive community points of view appears to be more important to the effectiveness of the school administrator than his evidencing similarity or congruence in viewpoint.

These studies bring insight into community expectations for the school and provide implications for the role of school administrators. If the principal and his staff are to work effectively with the various groups in their community, they must accurately perceive and understand group motivations and how they relate to expectations held by a group for the role of the school and the people who staff it.

The principal and the community. The extent to which a school principal can function effectively in his community is, in great measure, dependent upon a definition of his role that is mutally acceptable to himself and to the residents of his community. Achieving consensus on role, however, is difficult simply because of the differing perceptions and expectations of the people involved.

The fact that school communities differ requires administrators to be adaptable. The role played by a principal in one school may be totally inappropriate to another principal in a different school. Thus it appears that a universally applicable role-prescription is difficult, perhaps impossible, to formulate. Each principal must, in a sense, fashion his own role in light of several factors including the following:

1. There are many groups with which he must deal;
2. Each group has its own peculiar set of needs, desires, expectations and aspirations, as well as its own unique way of expressing them;
3. Groups vary significantly in educational viewpoint;
4. Groups will make different demands on him, each group in accordance with its own unique needs;
5. His own values and beliefs may be in conflict with those of his intra- and extra-organizational referents.

---

[37] Roderick F. McPhee, "Individual Values, Educational Viewpoint, and Local School Approval" *Administrator's Notebook*, Vol. 7, No. 8 (April 1959).

[38] Kenneth DeGood, "Can Superintendents Perceive Community Viewpoints" *Administrator's Notebook*, Vol. 8, No. 3 (November 1959).

The role, then, must be tailored to fit the unique constellation of community variables which form a school attendance area. It must be continuously under evaluation, and where necessary it must change.

Few communities remain the same for long. New residents, political realignments, and economic advance or decline all work to change the face of a community. Education also changes in response to increasing knowledge, emerging technology, and the developing psycho-social needs of the populace it serves.

The role of the principal must change as both the community and education itself change. If the principal is to meet the challenge of his position, he must lead in bringing those changes into meaningful combination. An important outlet for his leadership is through an effective school-community relations program. The details of such a program are discussed in Chapter VII.

CHAPTER III

Responsibilities of the Principalship: Overview

The preceding discussion of the role of the school principal pointed to the many varied and diffuse types of responsibilities he can have. Both his intraorganizational role and his extraorganizational role demand a wide range of activities and tasks.

A comprehensive list of critical task areas for school administrators has been developed by the Southern States Cooperative Program in Educational Administration.[1] It is reproduced here to illustrate the scope of the school administrator's responsibilities.

1. Critical Task Area: Instruction and Curriculum Development
   a. Providing for the formulation of curriculum objectives;
   b. Providing for the determination of curriculum content and organization;
   c. Relating the desired curriculum to available time, physical facilities, and personnel;
   d. Providing materials, resources, and equipment for the instructional program;
   e. Providing for the supervision of instruction;
   f. Providing for in-service education of instructional personnel.
2. Critical Task Area: Pupil Personnel
   a. Initiating and maintaining a system of child accounting and attendance;
   b. Instituting measures for the orientation of pupils;
   c. Providing counseling services;
   d. Providing health services;
   e. Providing for individual inventory service;
   f. Providing occupational and educational information services;
   g. Providing placement and followup services for pupils;
   h. Arranging systematic procedures for the continual assessment and interpretation of pupil growth;
   i. Establishing means of dealing with pupil irregularities;
   j. Developing and coordinating pupil activity programs;
3. Critical Task Area: Community School Leadership
   a. Helping provide an opportunity for a community to recognize its composition;

---

[1] Southern States Cooperative Program in Educational Administration, *Better Teaching in School Administration* (Nashville, Tenn.: George Peabody College for Teachers, 1955).

   b. Assisting a community to identify its potential for improvement through the use of natural and human resources;

   c. Determining the educational services;

   d. Helping to develop and implement plans for the improvement of community life;

   e. Determining and rendering services which the school can best provide in community improvement with and through the co-operation of other agencies;

   f. Making possible the continual re-examination of acceptable plans and policies for community improvement with particular reference to the services which the schools are rendering.

4. Critical Task Area: Staff Personnel

   a. Providing for the formulation of staff personnel policies;

   b. Providing for the recruitment of staff personnel;

   c. Selecting and assigning staff personnel;

   d. Promoting the general welfare of the staff;

   e. Developing a system of staff personnel records;

   f. Stimulating and providing opportunities for professional growth of staff personnel.

5. Critical Task Area: School Plant

   a. Determining the physical plant needs of the community and the resources which can be marshaled to meet those needs;

   b. Developing a comprehensive plan for the orderly growth and improvement of school plant facilities;

   c. Initiating and implementing plans for the orderly growth and improvement of school plant facilities;

   d. Developing an efficient program of operation and maintenance of the physical plant.

6. Critical Task Area: School Transportation

   a. Determining school transportation needs and conditions (roads, location of schools, and so on) under which transportation services must be rendered;

   b. Procuring equipment and supplies through approved methods of purchase and contract;

   c. Organizing and providing an efficient system of school transportation maintenance;

   d. Providing for the safety of pupils, personnel, and equipment;

   e. Developing an understanding and use of the legal provisions under which the transportation system operates.

7. Critical Task Area: Organization and Structure

   a. Establishing working relationships with local, state, and federal agencies to provide services needed by the school system;

   b. Working with the board of education in the formulation of school policy and plans;

   c. Designating appropriate operational units within the school system;

   d. Developing a staff organization as a means of implementing the educational objectives of the school program;

e. Organizing lay and professional groups for participation in educational planning and other educational activities.
8. Critical Task Area: School Finance and Business Management
   a. Organizing the business staff;
   b. Determining sources of school revenues;
   c. Formulating a salary schedule;
   d. Preparing the school budget;
   e. Administering capital outlay and debt service;
   f. Administering school purchasing;
   g. Accounting for school movies;
   h. Accounting for school property;
   i. Providing for a school insurance program;
   j. Providing for a system of internal accounting.[2]

The extent to which the school principal has responsibility for carrying out these tasks is, in the main, dependent upon the expectations held for him by his superior. A superior may delegate complete responsibility to the principal for the performance of certain tasks and retain for himself the responsibility for others. At the same time there may be certain tasks for which both the superior and the school principal may share responsibility. A study by Langlitz on the allocation of administrative functions between the chief school administrator and the secondary school principal illustrates the division of responsibility between these two positions.[3]

Delegated and Shared Tasks

Langlitz designed an instrument which contained 314 administrative functions. He asked 30 superintendents and the 30 secondary school principals who worked with them to check each function according to whether it was:

      1. Retained by the Chief School Administrator (CSA),
or 2. delegated to the High School Principal (HSP),
or 3. shared by the Chief School Administrator and the High School Principal (either as an equal sharing or as an unequal sharing).

He found that there was disagreement between the chief school

[2] *Ibid.*
[3] Harold N. Langlitz, "A Study of the Allocation of Administrative Functions between the Chief School Administrator and the Secondary School Principal in Selected Schools in New York State" (Doctoral dissertation, School of Education, Syracuse University, 1958). This study is reported in Council on Administrative Leadership, *Two Studies of Administrative Delegation* (Albany, N.Y.: The Council, March 1960).

administrator and the high school principal on nearly half of the total number of responses on allocation of function.[4] An important implication of this finding is that when the school principal and his superior do not each have a clear understanding of the other's functions, overlap—sometimes conflict—occur.

One way to avoid overlap of functions and the consequent potential for conflict is to develop job specifications for the school principal. Within each district the development of such specifications is an important shared function between the chief school administrator and the school principal. On the basis of the evidence in his study, Langlitz proposes the following ideal allocation of administrative functions between the chief school administrator and the secondary school principal.

Functions assigned to the secondary school principal.[5] The following functions are the delegated responsibility of the secondary school principal:

1. Accounting of pupils, census, and attendance;
2. Arranging for substitute teachers;
3. Assisting teachers in diagnosing learning difficulties of pupils;
4. Controlling pupil behavior;
5. Coordinating audio-visual activities;
6. Determining specifications for supplies and equipment;
7. Developing pupil reporting procedures;
8. Directing and coordinating the in-service training program;
9. Directing and supervising the pupil activity program;
10. Directing the guidance program;
11. Directing the health and safety program;
12. Directing the program for exceptional children;
13. Distributing supplies and equipment;
14. Helping teachers in planning effective remedial instruction;
15. Inducting and orienting nonprofessional staff personnel;
16. Inducting and orienting professional staff personnel;
17. Inventorying supplies and equipment;
18. Maintaining pupil personnel records;
19. Scheduling professional and nonprofessional staff personnel;
20. Scheduling pupils;
21. Supervising and auditing internal accounts;
22. Supervising nonprofessional staff personnel;
23. Supervising professional staff personnel.

Functions shared between the chief school administrator and

---

[4] *Ibid.*, pp. 218–219.
[5] *Ibid.*, pp. 233–237.

the high school principal.[6]   The following functions are suggested by Langlitz as being shared between the chief school administrator and the secondary school principal:

1. Conducting a research program;
2. Counseling professional and nonprofessional staff personnel;
3. Determining need and planning for plant expansion and renovation;
4. Directing program of plant maintenance;
5. Directing school lunch program;
6. Helping the board of education in determining the educational needs of the community;
7. Holding conferences with parents and other lay citizens;
8. Maintaining staff personnel records;
9. Making recommendations to the board of education for policy formulation and revision;
10. Planning and coordinating public relations program;
11. Preparing information to be disseminated by public communication media;
12. Rating, promoting, and dismissing nonprofessional staff personnel;
13. Rating, promoting, and dismissing professional staff personnel;
14. Recruiting and selecting nonprofessional staff personnel;
15. Recruiting and selecting professional staff personnel;
16. Revising the curriculum and selecting curriculum materials;
17. Working with PTA and other lay groups.

The list is by no means exhaustive, nor are all of the functions applicable in all cases. Functions could be added, subtracted, or altered in accordance with unique circumstances prevailing in a school district and also in accordance with the abilities of the individuals for whom the functions are intended.

An important factor to consider in outlining functions for the school principal is, that regardless of how inclusive the list might be, not all functions are of the same order of importance. Functions such as working with professional and non-professional staff, making policy recommendations, and working with the community are certainly not of the same order of importance as directing a school lunch program or maintaining staff personnel records. The study by Gross and Herriott reported that elementary school principals regarded the following as extremely or very important parts of their jobs:

1. Working on the improvement of curriculum;
2. Planning and conducting teachers' meetings;

---

[6] *Ibid.,* pp. 238–242.

3. Dealing with classroom problems of teachers;
4. Evaluating the performance of teachers;
5. Conferring with individual teachers;
6. Introducing new teaching methods;
7. Observing teachers in the classroom;
8. Coordinating the work of teachers;
9. In-service training.[7]

In devising a list of functions for the principal to perform, the principal and his superior must establish some hierarchy of importance with regard to the accomplishment of each function. Without such guidance the principal consciously or unconsciously could end up directing his energies almost exclusively to certain functions, totally neglecting others. The sheer number of tasks to be performed could swamp the principal causing him to be haphazardly wasteful of his energies and time.

Use of Time

If he is to successfully perform all the functions designated for his position, the principal must consider how he is going to use his time. Planning and allocation of time will enable the principal to achieve his goals in a systematic and organized manner. Without proper allocation of time, the efforts of the principal can become haphazard, often ending with tasks uncompleted and a sense of frustration at the inability to devote proper emphasis to important activities.

Many times the school principal will have to work at night to meet his responsibilities. Gross and Herriott report that over fifty per cent of the elementary school principals in their study worked an average of two to four nights a week.[8] They found also that the more off-duty time a principal devoted to his job the greater his Executive Performance Leadership score.[9] There may be something inherent in the job of the principal that necessitates his working at night, but it may well be that with the proper use of his on-the-job time he could limit the amount of off-duty time he has to spend.

A study of the use of time by selected high school principals in Oregon compared time actually spent on certain functions against opinions of authorities and principals on how time should be spent.

[7] Neal Gross and Robert E. Herriott, *The Professional Leadership of Elementary School Principals* (Washington, D.C.: The Cooperative Research Branch, Project No. 853, U.S. Office of Education, April 1964), Chapter 5, p. 18.

[8] *Ibid.,* Chapter 8, p. 6.

[9] *Ibid.,* p. 8. See also Chapter 2 of this book, footnote 5.

TABLE 1

Comparisons of Time Spent with Principals'
and Authorities' Opinions as to How Time
Should be Spent in the Secondary
Principalship[10]

	PERCENTAGE OF TIME		
	Authorities' Opinions	Principals' Opinions	Actually Spent
Category of Duties	N 29	N 204	N 62
Office Routine	9.7	12.9	22.5
Activity Program	8.7	9.2	17.8
Teaching	3.1	5.9	13.0
Supervision of Teachers and Improvement of Instruction	31.0	22.0	12.0
Pupil Personnel	11.1	14.5	8.4
Professional Meetings	5.6	3.7	6.6
Public Relations	9.7	6.7	5.6
Administration of the Plant	4.2	6.4	4.6
Superintendent's Conference	4.1	2.7	2.8
Business Management	5.7	7.8	2.7
School Board	2.1	3.2	2.2
Cafeteria	2.3	2.4	1.1
Transportation	2.8	2.6	0.7

This table provides an excellent illustration of what can happen when the use of time is not consciously planned. The authorities thought that almost one third of the high school principal's time should be spent for supervision of teachers and improvement of instruction. The high school principals in the study thought that approximately one fourth of their time should be spent for that activity. In actual practice, the principals spent less than one eighth of their time carrying it out. By contrast, the principals actually spent almost twice as much time in office routine than they thought they should.

A report of the time spent by elementary school principals on their major functions reveals that the amount of time allocated for each function has not changed much over a period of thirty years.[11] Elementary school principals report that they have spent approximately one third of their time for supervision and an equal amount of time for administration.

Allocating time. In a discussion on administration, Drucker

[10] Reprint of Table 1 in Harold V. McAbee, "Time for the Job," *NASSP Bulletin*, Vol. 42, No. 236 (March 1958) 41.
[11] National Education Association, *The Elementary School Principalship—A Research Study*, National Elementary Principal Bulletin 28, No. 1 (September 1958), 88.

points out that one of the basic rules which an effective administrator must observe is proper use of time. He says,

> There is no other resource like time. Time is utterly perishable and incapable of being restored, let alone of being manufactured in large supply. There is so much time—there is not going to be any more. And time once gone is gone forever. It is the scarcest and by far the most expensive resource we have—and usually the most thoroughly wasted one.[12]

The principal must recognize that his time is important and that if he is going to fulfill his role in the school and meet his professional obligations he must use it wisely. In this regard, Drucker makes the following comment:

> There may not be in the life of a busy administrator more than a few hours each week for which he can plan and which he can devote to the really important contributions he should make. All the more reason, therefore, to make sure that these hours are actually planned properly. Only by holding against each other the list of the truly important contributions and the time schedule can an administrator really make sure that the important things get done. If he either does not think through the contributions or does not know his time schedule, he is bound to give priority in time to the unimportant and to waste even the little time that is his to spend.[14]

In allocating his time properly the school principal must:

1. Clearly understand what his functions are;
2. Establish a set of priorities for completion of these functions;
3. Set a time schedule in light of these priorities;
4. Be flexible in adherence to this schedule while at the same time be resolved that only matters of importance will be allowed to contravene the previously established schedule.

Responsibilities in Perspective

The school principal has many responsibilities and professional obligations. His role calls for him to perform many duties spanning a variety of areas and touching upon diverse groups of people. Often many of these duties become menial, bothersome routine. Even more often the limitations of time prevent the principal from doing what he considers to be important. All of these factors and others can contribute to frustration and dismay. However, taken as a total-

---

[12] Peter F. Drucker, "The Effective Administrator," *NASSP Bulletin,* Vol. 48, No. 291 (April 1964), 160.
[14] *Ibid.,* p. 162.

ity and placed in proper perspective, the responsibilities of the principal come together in a meaningful pattern.

Each of the four chapters which follow describes in some detail one of the four major areas of concentration for the school principal.

CHAPTER IV

Principal's Functions: Developing the Educational Program

The central focus of all administrative effort should be upon the development of a program that will provide rich educational opportunities for each student. In most cases, major responsibility for developing such a program at the school building level is vested in the school principal. It is his responsibility to insure that the educational program in his school is as good as available sources permit.

Organizing for Instruction

In order to make efficient use of his professional staff, the principal must establish an organization for instruction that will achieve at least two purposes:

1. Establish and clarify the formal role-relationships among members of the staff by defining expectations for role performance and by setting the hierarchical arrangements so as to delineate authority and responsibility;
2. Lead in developing the operational framework within which the educational goals and objectives of the school may be expressed—grouping practices, teacher utilization procedures, and the like are the means by which the organization for instruction may be translated into action.

Clarifying role relationships. The concept of role has already been discussed in Chapter II, and much of that discussion is relevant to understanding the organization for instruction. The focus of this section will be upon the delineation of role relationships among certain positions in the instructional organization.

The type of structure provided for role clarification and delineation varies among schools. There are, however, two typical formats, one at the secondary the other at the elementary level. Figures 4–1 and 4–2 depict these formats. (See p. 39.)

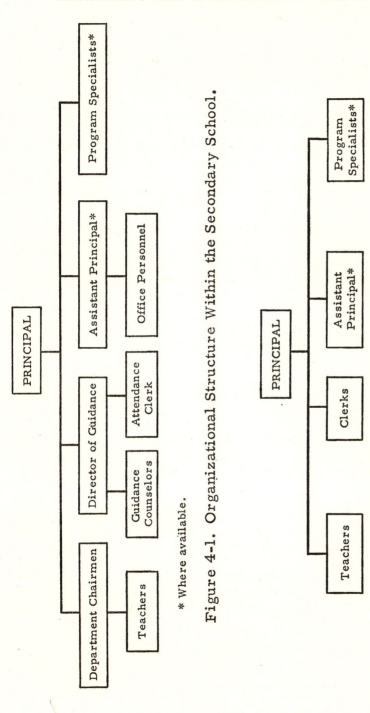

* Where available.

Figure 4-1. Organizational Structure Within the Secondary School.

* Where available.

Figure 4-2. Organizational Structure Within the Elementary School.

It should be clear from the illustrations above that many people are involved in making decisions affecting the instructional program. At the secondary school level for example, in addition to the principal the department chairman, the director of guidance, teachers, guidance counselors, and others in varying degree have a contribution to make to the planning of the instructional program. At the elementary school level, the situation is not as complex; there are fewer participants in the decision-making process. Also involved in this process are program specialists who are not assigned to a single school but who work out of a central office and serve many schools. These include supervisors, subject matter specialists, psychologists, and the like.

The potential for conflict in decision-making among the participants is ever present. Who decides what should be taught and how it should be taught is a question that can lead to acrimonious debate, disagreement, and open conflict. For example, it can be argued that the teacher should play the most important part in making decisions regarding the instructional program. This argument holds that because the teacher is closest to the learner, and because the teacher has the most-direct influence on whether the learner will benefit from the planned learning experiences, then it should be the teacher who determines the type of learning experiences that are to be provided. On the other hand, it can be argued that the program specialist should make the decisions about the instructional program because of his specialized knowledge. His expertise, it is argued, should give him license to determine the experiences to be provided the learner. These differences in point of view among the professional staff contain within them the seeds of conflict.

A key role in limiting the potential for conflict is played by the school principal. He must work to make clear to all parties concerned the role each must play. It is particularly important that he clearly delineate the role of the program specialist.

In most cases such specialists in education as curriculum coordinators, supervisors, and subject matter specialists are part of the central office staff. As such they are not members of a school staff, and a school's principal has no line of authority over them, except that specialists in reading or speech assigned to a particular school are under the authority of the principal.

A specialist on a central office staff does not have responsibility for making decisions regarding curriculum matters in a school. Decision-making is the prerogative of the school staff, and the principal must make this distinction clear. However, at the invitation of the school principal and his staff, the specialist may participate in the planning of the school program.

The specialist in education is as an important adjunct to the teacher role. His major function is to help teachers understand, interpret, and place into action the objectives of the school program. Through classroom visitation and observation and by consultation with the teacher, the specialist can assist the teacher to overcome weaknesses in teaching. The school psychologist, for example, may assist the teacher with a child whose learning is hampered by personal or family problems. It is in such ancillary ways that specialists in education make important contributions to the school program.

In describing the specialist's role to the staff, the principal must make explicit the fact that the specialist holds no line authority over teachers and cannot force them to carry out a suggestion. Both specialist and teacher must clearly grasp the professional limits within which they can interact. The principal must protect his teachers by seeing to it that these professional limits are not exceeded.

By attempting to maximize the contribution of each functional role in the instructional organization, the principal increases the potential for conflict among the role incumbents. His ability to keep this potential from erupting into open conflict is related to the confidence those under his authority have in his leadership. By making explicit his expectations for each role, and by being cognizant of the unique personality needs of each role incumbent, the principal enhances his chances for eliciting such confidence.[1]

Operational framework for the school program. The purpose of clarifying role relationships is to encourage each participant to make a maximum contribution within the operational framework established for the school program. Such a framework describes the means by which the school program is to be organized, and the practices by which that program are to be characterized. The following, for example, are related to the operational framework for the school program: (1) type of curriculum offered; (2) grouping practices; (3) grading practices; (4) organization of instructional teams; and (5) sequence of subjects and the like.[2]

---

[1] For a discussion on this topic see Chapter II.

[2] For a discussion of these and other topics see Association for Supervision and Curriculum Development, *Balance in the Curriculum* (Washington, D.C.: The Association, 1961). Also see Henry J. Otto and David C. Sanders, *Elementary School Organization and Administration* (New York: Appleton-Century-Crofts, 1964).

The framework established for organizing the learning experiences provided in a school program varies among schools. At least two important factors influence these variations; namely, the goals of the program and the opinions of the professional staff and others concerning the relative efficacies of certain frameworks, about the values of which there is considerable controversy. For example, there are some who suggest that elementary school programs should be organized according to a nongraded continuous-progress plan rather than by the traditional lock-step year-by-year advancement schedule. Evidence on the results of organizing an elementary school program according to the nongraded plan, however, is still quite inconclusive; many argue that its worth has yet to be proven.[3]

There are other frameworks which are characterized by such activities as team teaching, programmed instruction, and the like. Certain elements of each of these may be practical in many schools, but they are still sources of great controversy.

If he is to lead in the development of a framework suitable for his school, the principal must be thoroughly familiar with the pros and cons of each point of controversy. He can be of little or no use in resolving differences of opinion if he is not knowledgeable about the sources of them.

Once some agreement is reached regarding the type or types of framework believed desirable, the principal must be able to integrate the formulations suggested by experts and the opinions of his professional staff with his own perceptions of and expectations for the school program. To do this he must have a keen understanding of the totality of the school program—how each part in the program relates to every other part. More than any other person in his school, the principal must see to it that every piece in the instructional framework fits together into some meaningful and productive whole.[4]

---

[3] For a report of a study on the nongraded versus the graded plan of organization, see Robert F. Carbone, "The Nongraded School: An Appraisal" *Administrator's Notebook,* Vol. 10, No. 1 (September 1961).

[4] It is important to note that mere establishment of an organizational structure does not necessarily insure that the activities prescribed by this organization will be realized. Teachers, not structure, implement the program. For a discussion of how the principal works with teachers in implementing the program, see Chapter V.

Developing the Curriculum

Educational opportunity is related to the nature and quality of the learning experiences provided through the school curriculum. The curriculum includes consciously planned learning experiences with which the learner will be involved and which are designed to stimulate change in his behavior. A major task for the school principal is to provide leadership in developing a school curriculum that will include opportunities for each student to achieve his maximum learning potential. The principal's success in this role will depend, in part, upon his understanding of the many facets of curriculum development.

Determining goals. The first step in developing a curriculum lies in the determination of the goals. These goals provide the guidelines for the development of the curriculum and also "assure that the school is focusing its major attention upon important and significant ends rather than frittering away its time upon less imperative objectives."[5]

Curriculum goals must be planned to encompass the unique needs of the learner while at the same time reflecting the social demands of the community in which the learner lives. Smith points out that goals should be based upon a "sense of the social perspective which grows out of a continuing social analysis of an emerging society."[6] Setting such goals is an extremely complex process, involving many different people at varying levels of community life. Factors that are unique to the community setting also are important considerations in goal development.

Developing broad educational goals is a system-wide function but certain goals must be planned at the school level. In providing the leadership for goal-setting in his school, the principal must give consideration "to the ideas of youth, parents, and teachers as well as to all the factors, restrictive and otherwise, of facilities, system-wide plans, and pupil-teacher group proposals and reactions."[7] The two major functions of the school principal in this regard are (1) to provide an atmosphere wherein the principal, the teacher, and the community may study the needs of the learner and of society, and

---

[5] Ralph W. Tyler, "The Organization of Learning Experiences," in *Toward Improved Curriculum Theory*, Virgil E. Herrick and Ralph W. Tyler, eds. (Chicago: University of Chicago Press, 1950), p. 61.

[6] Ralph W. Tyler and Virgil E. Herrick, "Overview," *op. cit.*, p. 1.

[7] William M. Alexander "The Role of Leadership in Curriculum Planning," *op. cit.*, p. 103.

(2) to secure full expression by all parties involved, to guide discussion to group judgments, and to point out overlooked difficulties, goals, or relationships.[8]

Certain key questions must be asked by the principal concerning the goals that are being set. These questions include the following:

1. Are the goals suitable for the community and the school?
2. Are the goals appropriate in light of available personnel, facilities, and materials?
3. Do the goals provide explicit guides to the school program?
4. Do the goals relate to cognitive as well as to affective learnings?
5. Are the goals complete in terms of what may reasonably be expected of the learners in the school?

The answers to these key questions will point the direction the experiences to be provided through the educational program should take.

Planning learning experiences. The behavior of the learner, in large measure, is a function of his participation in and reaction to the learning experiences provided through the school program. These experiences represent what may be called the action part of educational goals.

Planning the types of learning experiences to be provided is a crucial task for the school staff. Under the leadership of the principal, the teachers select from among many possible alternatives the types of learning experience that will best express the goals of the program. To do this intelligently, they must have a clear conception of the nature of the desired learning experiences and the specific objectives to be realized through them. Four important factors underlying the desirability of learning experiences are (1) nature of the outcomes; (2) social demands; (3) learning and growth; and (4) cultural heritage.[9]

As with the setting of goals, the principal must ask certain questions regarding the appropriateness of the learning experiences. One such question concerns their vertical and horizontal relatedness: are the learning experiences repeated without alteration at different levels of the program, or are they in keeping with the varying expectations held for each level of the program? It would be quite wasteful of time, talent, and energy if, for example, the experiences provided in the third grade were to lead to the same learnings as

---

[8] *Ibid.,* p. 104.
[9] Gordon N. Mackenzie, "What Should be the Organizing Elements of the Curriculum?" in *Toward Improved Curriculum Theory, op. cit.,* pp. 54–57.

those provided in the second or the fourth grade. Similarly, it would be wasteful if the same types of experience were provided to slow learners as to fast ones.

A careful plan for articulating learning experiences would obviate such wasteful practices. It is the principal's responsibility to establish such articulation.

Providing resources. Closely allied with the planning of learning experiences is the need to provide resources to implement them. In many ways, the quality of a learning experience is directly related to the quality of the resources provided. Resources may be of two types: human, and material. Each requires the special attention of the school principal.

Material resources include textbooks, supplementary materials, equipment and supplies, and the like. As the designated head of the school, the principal is responsible for seeing that these materials are provided to the teachers, and this becomes one of the expectations which teachers will hold for the principal's role. In this respect the principal serves as facilitator for the teaching-learning process.

Too often available resources are quite limited, even inadequate. It is not uncommon to find teachers using outdated, worn textbooks and inadequate writing and reading equipment in rooms furnished with substandard chairs, desks, and tables. Under such circumstances the principal is forced to choose from among at least three alternative forms of behavior. He can, if he chooses, do nothing to improve the situation, hoping that all concerned will just learn to live with it. As perhaps the least consequence of that choice, his teachers may lose confidence in him and the program; worse, the students will certainly be deprived of opportunities for learning. Alternatively, the principal could make his needs known to the superintendent and insist upon improvement of the situation. But even vigorous protest cannot assure success, for the total resources of the entire school district may be limited.[10]

The third alternative presents the greatest challenge to the principal and his staff: they can use their collective ingenuity and creative talents to fashion resources in whatever way they can out of what is available. In this activity the principal contributes his own efforts, but more importantly he brings his teachers together with specialists who can provide vital assistance in preparing resources and can aid teachers to properly use them.

---

[10] Very often the only solution lies in increasing the tax base of the district through consolidation with other districts.

ending

No individual should be expected to be an expert in all areas of the school program and it is unrealistic to assume that, in all cases, the principal is best able to assist a teacher in solving educational problems. It is far more realistic to expect that the principal be able to work with the teacher to identify problem areas then, where feasible, to call upon the services of a specialist who can best help to solve the problem. Specialists who work, for instance, in such areas as art, music, physical education, and special services form what may be called *human resources* for the teacher.

Providing human and material resources for the school program is an important function for the school principal. He must take care that the resources which are provided maximally enhance the teaching and learning process. To this end the following guidelines are offered:

> 1. Greatest realization of the value of school dollars is achieved by providing liberally the relatively inexpensive materials which enhance sufficient use of the immeasurably more valuable time of teachers and children.
> 2. Official leadership is responsible for bringing to bear personnel resources from outside the system to assure breadth of viewpoint and to enrich and expand opportunities for professional growth.
> 3. Consultants and other supervisory personnel from the central office serve in individual buildings in cooperation with the principal and staff groups working on instructional problems. Services are available to all teachers and are generally most effective in improving teacher growth when rendered in response to expressed needs and requests for assistance.
> 4. Provisions of necessary resources requires that official leadership establish effective administrative procedures for their regular distribution and efficient utilization.[11]

Evaluating the Program

The purpose of evaluating the program is to ascertain the extent to which the stated goals of the school are being achieved. Changes in the school program should be introduced only as the products of a well planned on-going evaluation procedure.

Evaluation of the school program is a cooperative venture, carried on by the school principal, his staff, and other educational specialists where appropriate. The major emphasis is upon comparison of where the program is, against where the staff would like the

---

[11] Association for Supervision and Curriculum Development, *Leadership for Improving Instruction* (Washington, D.C.: The Association, NEA, 1960), p. 106.

program to be. Besides the implied need for change, this focus also seeks to maintain a maximally efficient relationship among the content to be learned, the known needs of learners, the available resources, and the competencies and skills of teachers.

There is some research evidence indicating that male principals tend to assess their programs somewhat differently than do female principals. A study by Gross and Trask attempted to find out whether female principals give greater weight than male principals do to individual differences among pupils.[12] The items used to test this notion were:

1. The degree to which special provisions are made for the "slow learner";
2. The degree to which special provisions are made for the "gifted child";
3. The degree to which teaching materials in addition to textbooks are being used;
4. The degree to which students work up to their capacities.[13]

The researchers found that female principals do incline to pay more attention to individual differences among pupils than do male principals.

Using related but different items, Gross and Trask found that:

1. Women view the presence of delinquency-prone pupils as a more important criterion in assessing schools than do men;[14]
2. Women place greater stress on a school's concern for the child's social and emotional development as a basis of evaluation than do men.[15]

More studies need to be done before definite conclusions are drawn as to how male and female principals differentially evaluate their programs. The significance of such differential evaluation to program formulation needs careful examination and documentation.

The principal must evaluate the program in his school for yet another reason. He must be able to report to the superintendent (and through the superintendent to the board of education) and to the school-community. The principal is constantly being asked questions about the appropriateness and the success of the program in his school. If he has established procedures for continuous pro-

---

[12] Neal Gross and Anne E. Trask, *Men and Women as Elementary School Principals* (Washington, D.C.: Cooperative Research Branch, U.S. Office of Education, Department of Health, Education, and Welfare, June 1964), Contract No. 853, Final Report No. 2.

[13] *Ibid.*, Chapter 5, p. 4.

[14] *Ibid.*, p. 17.

[15] *Ibid.*, p. 19.

gram evaluation, there will be available to him updated, current information which will enable him to report intelligently and at once on matters of school program.

Supervising the Program

The principal is ultimately responsible for the success of the program in his school. The many different yet related facets involved in achieving success make it necessary that the principal supervise the activities of the people who work in his building. Of primary importance is the supervision of the instructional program.

Definition and purpose. The major emphasis in supervision of the instructional program is upon the total setting for teaching and learning. Specifically, supervision of the instructional program refers to that dynamic enabling process by which a school program is made viable and through which the people responsible for the program are stimulated and helped to make best use of their knowledge and skills. Thus supervision of instruction encompasses all of the factors described in this chapter, and includes among its purposes (1) improvement of the teaching-learning situation, (2) improvement of teacher job satisfaction, (3) improvement of the curriculum, and (4) improvement of physical facilities.

Who supervises? Within any given school district may be found numbers of people who hold the title of *supervisor* or *curriculum consultant.* These program specialists, in the main attached to the central office, work through the school principal to assist the teachers on-the-job. Their titles notwithstanding, these supervisory specialists do not pre-empt the principal's responsibility for supervision. Within his own school, the principal is expected to supervise the program under his direction. How he views his supervisor role can have a direct influence upon the principal's success with this activity.

Gross and Trask asked elementary school principals to complete a self-evaluation questionnaire on several facets of their work. Using a rating scale which ranged from "Outstanding" to "Very Poor," the principals were instructed to self-rate their abilities on the following items:[16]

1. Getting experienced teachers to upgrade their performance;
2. Improving the performance of inexperienced teachers;
3. Getting teachers to use new educational methods;

---

[16] *Ibid.,* Chapter 6, p. 10.

4. Giving leadership to the instructional program;
5. Communicating the objectives of the school program to the faculty;
6. Getting teachers to coordinate their activities;
7. Knowing about the strengths and weaknesses of teachers;
8. Maximizing the different skills found in a faculty.

They found that women, on the average, set a higher value than men did on the ability to supervise in matters of instruction.[17] Using other related items, the researchers found that women find greater satisfaction in work related to instruction than men do.[18]

These findings point to the fact that in the area of supervision of instruction women tend to perceive themselves differently than men do. The perceptions the principal has of himself as supervisor of instruction will, in large measure, direct his behavior in influencing the school program. Where the principal does not view himself as playing an important role in supervision, there is the risk of deterioration of program and a lack of professional growth among the staff.

Perhaps the most important need for supervision lies in the area of professional growth of teachers. Through supervision, teacher strengths and weaknesses may be identified and remedial programs designed to overcome them. A continuous program of supervision is important to determine the type of assistance teachers need. How the principal works with the teacher and helps him grow professionally is discussed in the chapter which follows.

---

[17] *Ibid.*, p. 11.
[18] *Ibid.*, p. 18.

CHAPTER V

Principal's Functions:
Obtaining and Developing Personnel

Securing enough teachers to meet burgeoning student enrollments is a pressing problem continuously faced by educators. It is estimated that by 1970 a total of 2.1 million teachers will be needed, an increase of 40 per cent over the number in 1962.[1] Including teachers needed to meet increasing enrollment as well as replacements for those leaving the profession, it is estimated that 150,000 to 200,000 new teachers will be needed annually.[2]

The following tabulation gives the sources of demand for teachers nationally in 1963:[3]

1. To replace those leaving	130,000
2. To serve increasing enrollments	35,000
3. To relieve overcrowding and to eliminate part-time sessions	30,000
4. To give instruction and service not now provided	20,000
5. To replace the unprepared	20,000
Total need for 1963	235,000

The number of 1963 college graduates likely to enter teaching was estimated at 117,000, leaving an estimated net shortage of teachers for 1963 at 118,000.[4]

The gravity of this shortage is compounded by the fact that numbers alone do not adequately describe the supply-and-demand problem. The amount of preparation those entering the teaching profession have had varies considerably. Data from the 1960 U.S. Decennial Census reveal that 34.7 per cent of the teachers in public schools had completed five or more years of college, 45.0 per cent

---

[1] Joseph A. Kershaw and Roland N. Mekean, *Teacher Shortages and Salary Schedules* (New York: McGraw-Hill Book Company, Inc., 1962), p. 11.

[2] *Ibid.*

[3] National Education Association, Research Division, *Teacher Supply and Demand in Public Schools* (Washington, D.C.: The Association, Research Bulletin 1963), p. 20.

[4] *Ibid.*

had completed four years of college, but 20.3 per cent had completed less than four years of college.[5]

It is apparent from these data that the pool from which competent teachers may be selected is not only limited in numbers, it is also handicapped by varying levels of adequacy of preparation of those contained within it. These limitations lead to two rather imposing challenges for each school district: (1) how to obtain an adequate number of qualified teachers; (2) how to develop programs of in-service training to assist all teachers to achieve and maintain a high level of professional competency.

These challenges hold important implications for the roles of various administrators in the school system. In the main, however, they should be of greatest concern to the administrator who works most directly with the teachers—the school principal.

Teacher Selection

The actual hiring of a teacher is the prerogative of the board of education which, upon a favorable recommendation from the superintendent, usually will approve a contract for the new teacher. The selection of the teacher is the responsibility of the superintendent and members of his staff selected to assist him in this task. For the most part, superintendents draw assistance in the task from central office personnel, relying only to a limited degree on their principals.

Principal involvement. The evidence on the true extent to which today's principal is involved in teacher selection is quite meager. Dean, however, reports that in only approximately 18 per cent of his sample of schools were elementary school principals carrying a responsibility for staff selection.[6]

Gross and Herriott in their study of elementary school principals asked principals "How frequently does the higher administration . . . allow a principal to evaluate teaching applicants who are being considered for appointment to your school?"[7] They found that "of the 164 principals who gave usable responses, 18 (11 per cent) said,

[5] *NEA Research Bulletin* (Washington, D.C.: Division of Research, National Education Association) Vol. 42, No. 3 (October 1964).

[6] Stuart E. Dean, *Elementary School Administration and Organization* (Washington, D.C.: U.S. Department of Health, Education and Welfare Bulletin OE 23006, No. 11, 1960), 89–94.

[7] Neal Gross and Robert E. Herriott, *The Professional Leadership of Elementary School Principals* (Washington, D.C.: Cooperative Research Project No. 853, U.S. Office of Education, April 1964).

'almost always'; 35 (21 per cent) said 'occasionally'; 41 (25 per cent) said 'almost never'; and 37 (23 per cent) said 'never.' "[8] The researchers found too that the more the higher administration involves a principal in the selection of his teachers the greater is his Executive Performance Leadership score.[9] It appears from this finding that a principal is in better position to offer leadership to those teachers in whose selection he was directly involved.

The need to involve principals more directly in the selection of teachers has become more apparent in recent years. The principal must work with the teacher, and it is he who is ultimately held responsible for the achievement of the teachers in his building, hence it is held reasonable he should play an important role in teacher selection. The American Association of School Administrators (AASA) makes this point:

> School systems will continue to vary widely in the degree to which they involve principals and classroom teachers in the selection process. Ideally several persons should participate. Since principals have a big stake in the outcome they should have a voice in the choice of candidates.[10]

The practice of denying the principal a direct role in selecting teachers does not entirely eliminate him from the selection process. Before embarking on a recruitment program, most school systems call upon the principal to provide information on how many new teachers will be needed in his building and what professional competencies they should have. Through his answers the principal in a measure influences the selection of candidates to be interviewed.

Teacher Orientation

It becomes the principal's responsibility to orient a newly-appointed teacher assigned to his building. To achieve this the principal must acquaint the appointee with such matters as the school program, the school's operating procedures, and his expectations for the teacher's role. The appointee must become acquainted with his colleagues and with the community. If the appointee is an experienced teacher, the orientation required need not be as intensive as that required for an appointee who is new to the teaching pro-

---

[8] *Ibid.*, pp. 6–18.
[9] *Ibid.* See also Chapter II of this book, footnote 5.
[10] American Association of School Administrators, *Staff Relations in School Administration* (Washington, D.C.: Thirty-third Yearbook of the Association, 1955), p. 35.

fession, who may indeed present a very special challenge to the principal.

Every year teacher-training institutions throughout the country graduate thousands of people who will enter the teaching field for the first time. These new teachers, in the main, are in their early twenties and will be undertaking their first full-time jobs. His experience during his first teaching assignment will in many ways condition the future efficiency and success of the teacher in his chosen field. It is not uncommon to find that many new teachers leave the field at the end of their first year of teaching because they are unable to cope with the problems inherent in a new and demanding situation. These teachers make early surrender to problems which, faced alone, prove overwhelming.

Problems of new teachers. In a recent survey of personnel practices in the New York City Public Schools, interviews with teachers revealed the following:

> Many teachers indicated that their first year was filled with bewilderment. Problems relating to completing forms, keeping attendance records, knowing the students and the community, and coping with poor working conditions were those most frequently mentioned by the interviewees as areas where they most needed assistance during their first year. One teacher summed it up when she said, "Nobody can really teach during the first year . . . you've got to learn how to plan your lessons, handle the kids, do all the clerical work . . . I used to come home exhausted at the end of every day."[11]

New teachers rarely begin their teaching service at the peak of efficiency. After his years in college, the neophyte teacher embarks on his new career and encounters problems not anticipated by even the best of teacher-training courses. A review of the literature reveals that there are eight general areas within which the problems encountered by new teachers may be grouped:

1. Problems related to understanding the school's philosophy and objectives, procedures and routines;
2. Problems related to conditions of work;
3. Problems related to control over pupils;
4. Problems involving provisions for individual differences;

---

[11] Daniel E. Griffiths *et al., Teacher Mobility in New York City: A Study of the Recruitment, Selection, Appointment and Promotion of Teachers in the New York City Public Schools* (New York: School of Education, New York University, 1963), p. 57. See also Daniel E. Griffiths, Samuel Goldman, and Wayne McFarland, "Teacher Mobility in New York City," *Educational Administration Quarterly* Vol. 1, No. 1 (Winter 1965).

5. Problems related to pupil motivation;
6. Problems involving teacher-community relationships;
7. Problems related primarily to instruction;
8. Problems related to evaluation.[12]

The problems commonly experienced by teachers in their first teaching assignment give evidence there is need for an induction program for new teachers. Planning and organizing such a program is a major responsibility of the school principal. Through a well-planned orientation program the principal can help his newly-appointed faculty member overcome problems which are experienced in the school and community. Such a program should include:

1. An introduction to the community;
2. An introduction to the school;
3. Discussion of instructional problems which may be of importance to the new teacher.[13]

The orientation program may be organized in a number of ways (e.g., by grade level or by department), and representatives from all levels, including central office personnel and teachers, should be involved. Often the principal will assign an experienced *helping* or *buddy teacher* to the neophyte who will help him cope with routine problems that may arise.

Whatever the format for the orientation program, the important factor for the principal to note is that it is his responsibility to provide the means whereby the new teacher will become a satisfied, efficiently-functioning member of the faculty. The orientation program should last long enough to guide the new teacher smoothly into the school's in-service training program.

Teacher Evaluation

The findings of an NEA survey on teacher evaluation[14] reveal that "The person chiefly responsible for evaluating teachers is the principal"[15]—no great revelation, for evaluation is an integral part

---

[12] Samuel Goldman, "The Orientation of New Teachers to the School" (Master's thesis, Department of Education, University of Chicago, 1958), p. 48.

[13] For a more complete discussion of orientation programs for new teachers see G. G. Eye and W. R. Lane, *The New Teacher Comes to School* (New York: Harper & Bros., 1956).

[14] National Education Association Research Division, *Evaluation of Classroom Teachers* (Washington, D.C.: The Association, Research Report R–14, December 1964).

[15] *Ibid.*, p. 73.

of the principal's over-all responsibility in developing his school staff. The principal must evaluate teachers because he must collect data which are important to decisions related to:

1. Retention of probationary teachers;
2. Assignment of specific tasks and duties;
3. Types of in-service programs needed;
4. Improving instructional procedures;
5. Salary increments.

Evaluation is a crucial factor in his career, for all written evaluative statements become part of the personnel file that follows the teacher wherever he goes. Because it is so crucial, many principals call upon others within the system to assist in evaluating a teacher. The survey on teacher evaluation reports that:

> In the elementary schools, of those principals making written evaluations of probationary teachers, 36.2 per cent shared the responsibility with the instructional supervisor; 23.8 per cent with the superintendent; 8.7 per cent with department heads; and 8.0 per cent with the assistant principal. In the secondary schools, of those principals making written evaluations of continuing teachers, the responsibility was shared by 33.0 per cent with the superintendent; 32.4 per cent with the assistant principal; 29.8 per cent with instructional supervisors; and 23.9 per cent with department heads.[16]

Criteria for evaluation. How teachers should be evaluated has been a source of great controversy. In recent years, the concept of merit rating has been debated widely. It is argued by many that since teachers are not all of the same caliber, the better teachers should enjoy greater rewards, financial and otherwise, than should the poorer teachers. Others argue that merit rating inhibits teachers from sharing ideas and causes jealousies among them. Parents also would cause problems by demanding that their children be taught only by the better teachers, it is argued.

Perhaps the most significant aspect of the controversy centers around conflicting opinions on how one measures quality of teaching. Should teachers be judged on the basis of their own performance in the classroom, or should they be judged on the basis of the performance of their students? Should the personality of the teacher be a factor in evaluation? There is little agreement on the part of those who do the evaluating on precisely what dimensions of teacher performance are important in quality teaching. In a study of ele-

---

[16] *Ibid.,* p. 73. The figures reported are approximately equal for both probationary and continuing teachers.

mentary school principals, Gross and Trask found that men and women emphasize different criteria for the evaluation of teachers.[17] The researchers found that:

1. Women attribute greater importance than do men to the teachers' technical skills as a measure of how they carry out their work.[18]
2. Women emphasize the teachers' organizational responsibility as a criterion for evaluating their performance more strongly than do men.[19]

Often a principal and his teaching staff will devise a scale by which the teacher can be evaluated, usually expressed as a list of behaviors which are clearly defined, easily observed, and objectively ratable. With this list both the teacher and the principal know the expected behaviors being rated.

While this technique of teacher rating seems to be the easiest and most objective, it nonetheless does not avoid subjectivity. It is still the principal who has to see the behavior, interpret and rate it. Because this is unavoidable, it places a tremendous obligation upon the principal to be as fair and as impartial as possible.

Discussing the evaluation.   In order that evaluation serve as an effective tool for professional growth, the principal must review his rating of a teacher with that teacher. No principal should be out to "get" a teacher through rating. The objective is to assist the teacher through a rating device which highlights perceived strengths and weaknesses.

Once a rating is made, it is incumbent upon the principal to show the teacher the rating he received. An NEA survey on teacher evaluation reports, however, that in the study sample more than one teacher in four indicated that they did not see their evaluations at all.[20] This practice obviates the most important purpose of evaluation. Without being able to discuss with his principal his weaknesses in teaching performance, a teacher will not know where he needs professional upgrading. Furthermore, by denying the teacher knowledge about how he is rated, the principal can stir up feelings of resentment, suspicion, and fear in the teacher. Often these feelings militate against a sound, professional relationship between teacher and principal. When such a poor relationship exists the teacher does

---

[17] Neal Gross and Anne E. Trask, *Men and Women as Elementary School Principals* (Washington, D.C.: Cooperative Research Branch, Project No. 853, U.S. Office of Education, June 1964).

[18] *Ibid.,* Chapter 5, p. 30.

[19] *Ibid.,* p. 31.

[20] National Education Association Research Division, *Evaluation of Classroom Teachers* (Washington, D.C.: The Association, Research Report R–14, December 1964), p. 53.

not grow professionally and the instructional program is weakened.

It must be stressed that the major purpose behind teacher-rating is improvement of instructional competence. Open and frank discussion between the principal as rater and the teacher as the one rated is important if this purpose is to be achieved.

It is further important that the principal follow up the discussion of his rating with the teacher at a later date. Remedial action may have been warranted by the rating and it is the principal's responsibility to assist the teacher in obtaining the necessary help, perhaps in the form of course work at a university, observation of classroom teaching, or attendance at in-service workshops.

Suggestions on rating.   There is little doubt but that the evaluation of teachers can be a potential source of conflict between teacher and principal, especially if the criteria and procedures for evaluation are not clear. The need to make evaluation as positive an experience as possible suggests that rating procedures be carefully developed. Linder and Gunn offer the following suggestions to assist the principal in rating his staff:

1. Methods used in rating should be as objective and scientific as possible to influence the subjective elements which are inescapable.

2. The results of ratings should be given to teachers in written form. Any written document on rating that is to be placed in the teacher's permanent file and which becomes a public record should be read and signed by him.

3. Rating results should give each person rated some concrete basis for the improvement of his efficiency as a teacher.

4. There should be a mutual agreement between the administrative and the teaching staffs on the rating instrument to be employed. If the instrument has been previously established, there should be agreement on the interpretation of its separate items. The practices in applying the instrument should be understood by all to whom the rating procedure applies.

5. As far as possible, the emphasis in rating should be directed at the teaching results rather than at the teacher as a person.

6. Rating should be performed consistently and regularly to eliminate the necessity of emergency rating to determine a teacher's status.

7. Cumulative records should be maintained on each teacher rated and the interrelations of separate ratings should be studied.

8. Since self-evaluation is the best and most effective form of rating, the teacher should be encouraged to rate himself and compare the results with those of the principal. Any tendency for the teacher to overrate or to underrate himself can provide a significant basis for discussion.

9. It should be the aim of the principal to make the rating conference as relaxing as possible. Effort should be made to dispel any undue tension.

10. Honesty and frankness in rating are twin obligations of the principal. If good schools are to be maintained, the incompetent teacher must not be protected nor the superior teacher underrated because of a vague perfectionism amounting to official prejudice.[21]

Teacher Growth and Development

The major objective of in-service training programs is to stimulate and provide the means for the professional growth and development of teachers. Such a program, well planned and organized, can prove invaluable, not only in improving the professional competencies of the teacher, but also in upgrading the educational program of the school.

Professional growth of teachers may find expression through any and all of the following areas:

1. Improved knowledge of subject matter;
2. Improved techniques for teaching;
3. Better insight into the dynamics of teaching and learning;
4. Better understanding of self;
5. Better understanding of the learner;
6. Better relations with other teachers and administrators in the school system;
7. Better understanding of expectations for the teacher role;
8. Better understanding of the professional obligations of teachers.

Each of these areas should at some point be incorporated into an in-service training program for the staff.

In-service programs. To be effective, the in-service program should be based upon a careful identification of the professional needs of the teacher. A good source of data for this is an evaluation of the teacher's performance by the principal and the teacher. These data can serve to identify teacher strengths and weaknesses, providing the basis for planning specific types of in-service programs. Other data sources include classroom visitations, consultations with teachers and supervisors, and identification of teacher needs by outside consultants. Teachers, supervisors, outside consultants, and principals may all be involved in planning the in-service program, but the responsibility for leadership in the establishment and maintenance of the program rests largely with the school principal.

The content of a suitable in-service program will differ from one school to another, each being a response to the leadership propensi-

[21] Ivan H. Linder and Henry M. Gunn, *Secondary School Administration: Problems and Practices* (Columbus, Ohio: Charles E. Merrill Books, Inc., 1963), pp. 126–127.

ties of a principal and the unique needs of his staff. Following are some activities which a principal might promote for the in-service development of his staff:

1. Classroom visitation by the principal, supervisor and/or subject matter specialists. Through careful observation by the principal or by a trained specialist of the on-the-job performance of teachers, strengths and weaknesses can be identified and remedies prescribed.
2. Individual conferences to discuss problems and to seek solutions.
3. Faculty meetings to explore problems of mutual concern.
4. Specially instituted in-service seminars to study specific problems facing teachers.
5. Intervisitation among classrooms or schools. Such an experience could enable teachers to observe master teachers in action.
6. Encouragement to carry on a program of advanced study at a university.
7. Action research to permit the staff to gain a better understanding of local school and community problems and to provide evidence for possible change.

In planning in-service programs of any type the school principal must be sensitive to the close relationship between improvement of the educational program, professional growth, and the satisfaction of the personal needs of each teacher. Perhaps no other factor can do more to promote or impede professional growth than the on-the-job satisfaction among teachers in a school.

Teacher job satisfaction. Through research, certain factors have been identified which seem to have some relationship to teacher job satisfaction. Chase found the state of teacher satisfaction to be affected by participation in the planning and formulation of policy.[22] Bidwell confirmed Chase's finding and added that:

1. Teacher job satisfaction increases when current practices in decision-making conform to the practices most acceptable to the teacher;
2. Teachers are most satisfied with administrators who fulfill the expectations of their staff.[23]

Khalil studied teachers' perceptions of their principal's role in maintaining the morale of the faculty. He found the most important factors to be:

1. Personal qualities of the principal;
2. Effective communication to and from teachers;

---

[22] Francis S. Chase, "Factors for Satisfaction in Teaching," in *Phi Delta Kappa* 33:127–32 (1951).
[23] Charles E. Bidwell "The Administrative Role and Satisfaction in Teaching," in *Journal of Educational Sociology,* 29:41–47 (1955).

3. Provision for opportunities of teacher participation in formulating policies and decisions;
4. Support of teachers;
5. Professional behavior;
6. Maintenance of high standards through effective organization.[24]

These studies provide evidence which indicates that teachers who actively participate in the decision-making process exhibit greater job satisfaction than do those to whom such opportunity has been denied. The obvious implication for the principal's behavior is that he should involve his teachers in making decisions which affect them, certainly in planning in-service programs.

Some teachers, for whatever their reasons, will refuse to discuss their problems with the principal or to become intimately involved in planning an activity even though it be designed to solve some of their problems. These teachers may fear that admitting to a weakness will predispose an unfavorable evaluation. Such behavior may be viewed as a symptom of "closed organizational climate," a situation within the school which operates to impede the staff's feeling that teachers are free to express themselves.

Organizational climate. Argyris defined *organizational climate* as a "living complexity composed of three related systems of variables: formal organizational procedures, personal needs, and the complicated pattern of variables' associated with the individual's efforts to accommodate his own needs with those of the organization.[25] Halpin and Croft define it as the "personality of a school."[26] They distinguish six organizational climate profiles:

1. *The Open Climate* describes an energetic, lively organization which is moving towards its goals, and which provides satisfaction for the group members' personal needs. Leadership acts emerge easily and appropriately from both the group and the leader. The members are preoccupied disproportionately with neither task achievement nor social needs satisfaction; satisfaction on both counts seems to be obtained easily and almost effortlessly. The main characteristic of this climate is the "authenticity" of the behavior that occurs among all the members.

2. *The Autonomous Climate* is described as one in which leadership acts emerge primarily from the group. The leader exerts little

---

[24] Geji I. Khalil, "Principals' Role in Developing Staff Morale," in *The High School Journal* 46:81–91 (December 1962).

[25] Chris Argyris, "Some Problems in Conceptualizing Organizational Climate: A Case Study of a Bank," in *Administrative Science Quarterly,* II (March 1958), 501–520.

[26] Andrew Halpin and Don Croft, *The Organizational Climate of Schools* (Chicago: Midwest Administration Center, University of Chicago, 1963).

control over the group members; high *esprit* results primarily from social needs satisfaction; satisfaction from task achievement is also present, but to a lesser extent.

3. *The Controlled Climate* is characterized best as impersonal and highly task-oriented. The group's behavior is directed primarily toward task accomplishment, while relatively little attention is given to behavior oriented to social-needs satisfaction. *Esprit* is fairly high, but it reflects achievement at some expense to social-needs satisfaction. This climate lacks openness, or "authenticity" of behavior, because the group is disproportionately preoccupied with task achievement.

4. *The Familiar Climate* is highly personal, but undercontrolled. The members of this organization satisfy their social needs, but pay relatively little attention to social control in respect to task achievement. Accordingly, *esprit* is not extremely high simply because the group members secure little satisfaction from task achievement. Hence, much of the behavior within this climate can be construed as "inauthentic."

5. *The Paternal Climate* is characterized best as one in which the principal constrains the emergence of leadership acts from the group and attempts to initiate most to these acts himself. The leadership skills within the group are not used to supplement the principal's own ability to initiate leadership acts. Accordingly, some leadership acts are not even attempted. In short, little satisfaction is obtained in respect to either achievement or social needs; hence, *esprit* among the members is low.

6. *The Closed Climate* is characterized by a high degree of apathy on the part of all members of the organization. The organization is not "moving"; *esprit* is low because the group members secure neither social-needs satisfaction nor the satisfaction that comes from task achievement. The members' behavior can be construed as "inauthentic"; indeed, the organization seems to be stagnant.[27]

As a means for examining the "personality" of a school, Halpin and Croft developed the *Organization Climate Description Questionnaire* (O.C.D.Q.). Analysis of responses to the O.C.D.Q., can provide insight into the type of leadership exercised by a school's principal. For example, Feldvebel used the O.C.D.Q. and found that two of the sub-tests in it—Production Emphasis and Consideration, both related to the principal's leadership behavior—correlated significantly with pupil achievement level.[28] This finding points to the strong leadership influence the principal can have directly upon the teacher and, thereby, indirectly upon the learner.

[27] Andrew Halpin and Don Croft, "The Organizational Climate of Schools," *Administrator's Notebook*, Vol. XI, No. 7 (March 1963).

[28] Alexander M. Feldvebel, "Organizational Climate, Social Class and Educational Output," *Administrator's Notebook*, Vol. XII, No. 8 (April 1964).

All research on organizational climates in schools is relatively recent. Preliminary findings, however, seem to support the notion that a measure of school climate is a useful means for understanding the leadership acts of the principal and for assessing the opportunities for growth and development of teachers in his school.

CHAPTER VI

Principal's Functions:
School-Community Relations

A unique characteristic of American public schools is the participation of people at the local level, who through legally established channels of government in large measure influence almost every aspect of the educational program. It may well be said that it is primarily in direct response to the support afforded by the citizenry that the public schools function.

A major task of school administrators is to keep the public well informed of school activities so that it, the public, may make wise decisions about education and so that positive support will continue. Keeping the public informed and actively interested in school affairs is the purpose of a school-community relations program.

Definition and Need

School-community relations define the mutual understandings of school program and community needs which exist between the professionals who work in the schools and the citizens who support them. These understandings are necessary if the school is to reflect the values of the community and also be a positive influence on the future directions of it. If the American system of education is to continue to operate on this principle, the relationship between the schools and the community must be maintained at its highest level.

Historically, the need for an effective program of school-community relations became evident when professionals began to have major responsibility for school programs. In the early nineteenth century, supervision of the public schools was a function of the town government. "Policies were determined in the town meeting and the selectmen performed the administrative duties necessary to the operation of schools and other town agencies."[1] In this way public

---

[1] Stephen J. Knezevich, *Administration of Public Education* (New York: Harper & Bros., 1962), p. 215.

policies become school practice. However, as the responsibility for planning and supervising public education came to be placed in the hands of professional educators, the general public began to lose direct contact with the schools. The gap in mutual understanding between the school and its public caused problems.

There soon arose a recognition of the need for better communication between the school and the public it served.[2] Newspapers began to devote space to school activities; schools sent out news bulletins to parents and to taxpayers; parent-teacher associations were developed; the room-mother system was developed; service and civic clubs interested themselves in the schools; and adult-education programs were started. Professional educators further recognized the need for a precision of language by which the public could better understand the purposes of the school program. "School administrators and teachers discovered that if a proposal had definite merit, it would be accepted by the community, provided that it was explained in simple terms."[3]

The current practice in many school systems is to have well-developed public relations programs emanating from the central office. In the main, the superintendent is responsible for these programs, although in recent years many of the larger systems have appointed special directors of public relations. Much of a school-community relations program at the local level, however, is the responsibility of the school principal.

In carrying out his school-community relations program, the principal must define his school-community. He cannot simply regard the parents of the children who attend his school as comprising his entire community, for there are people with no children attending school who live within the environment and are important to the support of the school program.

The concept of community is very complex. Yeager suggests that a fruitful way of looking at the community is in terms of its structural and functional aspects. He says:

> The structure of the community may be described in terms of its geographical location, its legal boundaries, its occupations, service institutions, historical past, face-to-face contacts, centers of interest,

---

[2] For a discussion on this point see Myles W. Rodehaver, William B. Axtell, and Richard E. Gross, *The Sociology of the School* (New York: Thomas Y. Crowell, 1957), pp. 203–207.

[3] *Ibid.*, p. 207.

and form of government. . . . The structural description does not, however, convey the interactive nature of community living. This can best be explained functionally, that is, through the interactions and associations of individuals and groups as they live together. Human associations may take such forms as the family, clusters of families in neighborhoods, and established institutions such as churches, trade unions, political groups, social agencies. . . . The level of community living may best be determined through the nature, quality, and influence of its functional living.[4]

Thus the principal's school community is comprised of those people who live in an area which is contiguous with the school, people who have some common purposes expressed through associations, and who in some way can have a more or less direct influence on the school program.

Factors in the School-Community Relations Program

It may be accepted as a given fact that a majority of the public has a generally favorable attitude toward public education. There are, however, always some who for religious, political, economic, or other reasons oppose the public school programs offered in their areas. The principal must know who these people are, and he must understand the nature and the magnitude of their opposition. He cannot afford the luxury of working with his supporters to the neglect of his opposition. Both should be important foci of his school-community relations program.

Perhaps the three groups most important to the principal as he carries out his school-community relations program are teachers, students, and parents.

Teachers and the school image. The behavior and performance of the teachers will, in large measure, influence the image the public will have of the school. In actual practice, much of a community's reaction to the school program will come as a direct consequence of what the teachers do in their day-to-day work in the classroom. Parents generally evaluate a school in terms of the success of teachers' efforts to educate their children, as Van Winkle observed in a study of school-community information programs:

> When asked what they liked most about their schools, parents named teachers to a much greater extent than any other aspect of

---

[4] William A. Yeager, *School-Community Relations* (New York: The Dryden Press, 1951), p. 439.

the schools. They named teachers, it is felt, because of the very close relationship that exists between the teachers and their children.[5]

Teachers also influence the school image in ways other than through their direct contact with children. Through their written communications sent to the home, their personal contacts with parents, and through their over-all behavior in the community, teachers establish an image of themselves and, by extension, an image of the school. Undesirable behavior on the part of the teachers reflects negatively on the total school program and adversely affects the community's support for it. In many ways the teachers are among the most-scrutinized representatives of the school, and how they are viewed by the public will influence public opinions about the school.[6]

Because they play such an important role in creating the image of the school, teachers should be involved in planning and implementing such school-community relations activities as open-house programs, PTA-sponsored events, and conferences with parents. Teachers so involved are kept aware of the many and diverse elements of a public relations program and are alert to contributions they might make to strengthen it.

Students and school-community relations. Perhaps the most crucial element in the entire school-community relations program is the student, for he constitutes the strongest, most influential link between the community and the school. The attitudes, impressions, and values which students take home from their classes affect the attitudes, impressions, and values their parents and the community at large will formulate with regard to the school. Van Winkle points out that well over half the parents in his study identified their children as the source from which they received information about the schools.[7] This finding has important implications for the type of school-community relations program a principal should plan.

---

[5] Harold Van Winkle, "Good Schools Tell Their Story," in *Administrator's Notebook,* Vol. 5, No. 4 (Chicago: Midwest Administration Center, The University of Chicago, December 1956).

[6] It may be suggested that one reason some teachers prefer to teach in large city school systems is that they are not easily visible to the public after school hours. The bigness of the city affords a teacher an opportunity to separate his private from his professional life, a separation much more difficult to achieve in smaller school districts where there is a greater opportunity for teachers to be visible to the public. This is especially true for teachers who live in the community in which they also teach. It is not uncommon to hear these teachers refer to themselves as leading a goldfish-bowl existence because of their constant visibility in the community.

[7] *Ibid.*

Van Winkle points out that "the principal interest of the great majority of parents in their schools lies in their children and in whatever most closely affects their children, regardless of the kind or extent of information program carried on by the school."[8] Devices of communication such as school letters, bulletins, and school newspapers do not produce the same kind or magnitude of effect in parents as do the reactions of their children to the educational program, as Van Winkle points out: "Parents are much more interested in their schools in terms of their children than they are in terms of buildings and books and budgets."[9]

The school principal, therefore, in planning his school-community relations program, does well to emphasize the child as both a communicator and a focal point.

Parent and school support.   Perhaps the group of noneducators of greatest significance for the principal is the group of parents whose children attend his school. It is the parent who, on the basis of his impressions of how well his child is progressing in the program, has the potential to be most active as a supporter or detractor of the school. Parents can be helpful through work on school committees, in the PTA, or assisting teachers with special projects. Through positive expressions of support the school program and teachers, parents can also develop in their homes a positive attitude towards education on the part of their children, creating a respect for learning that will greatly aid the teaching and learning process. Parents also are important determinants of the degree of support which a principal will obtain from the community-at-large for the program in his school.

In recognition of the importance parents have in the school-community relations program, the principal must make every effort to increase parent interest and participation in the activities of the school. The Association for Supervision and Curriculum Development makes the following suggestions for inspiring such parent participation:[10]

1. Complete educational development in a community will include a program of parent education.

2. A great opportunity in most school systems is the induction of young parents into their new role in education when their first child enters school.

---

[8] *Ibid.*
[9] *Ibid.*
[10] Association for Supervision and Curriculum Development, *Forces Affecting American Education* (Washington, D.C.: The Association, 1953), p. 151.

3. If we had to settle for only one parent-school relationship, we should take a program of arranged conferences between the parents of a child and his teacher or teachers. . . . Boards of education, administrators and teacher groups should work out ways to make such a program an integral part of the school system and its activities.

4. Teachers to whom children are assigned on a full-time basis in an elementary school or on a core or homeroom basis in the junior and senior high schools should be responsible for organizing a series of from four to six meetings a year involving all parents of the children assigned to them . . . these arrangements will give parents and teachers a chance to exchange ideas and develop understandings about the content and methods that are used in different grades, in different subjects, and at different maturity levels.

5. The community-wide organizations of parents, such as the parent-teacher associations and parent councils, serve a very important function. Such organizations can and do accept exceedingly significant community, state, and nation-wide responsibilities for the welfare of the schools. The parent-teacher organization is the most useful and potentially powerful lay organization cooperating with the public schools in this country.

The Principal and School-Community Relations

The principal must know and understand his community thoroughly. He must study it by deriving and comprehending data from such questions as:

1. What is the general community level of approval or disapproval of this school program?

2. What kind of educational philosophy does the community hold?

3. What kind of prestige do teachers as an educational class hold in the community?

4. What kind of community is this with regard to such characteristics as cohesiveness and unity of action?

5. How does the community define the role of the school administrator?

6. How receptive is this community to change and innovation?[11]

Studying the community to seek answers to these and other relevant questions should be a continuing activity carried on by the principal and his professional staff. The school-community relations program should be planned and implemented in the light of these answers.

Building relationships between school and community is not a

---

[11] Robert P. Bullock, *School-Community Attitude Analysis for Educational Administration,* SCDS Monograph No. 7 (Columbus, Ohio: Ohio State University, 1959).

one-shot effort, hastily contrived to overcome some unfavorable community reaction. It is rather an on-going activity designed to bind the school and the community together in a mutually rewarding educative activity. A positive relationship between the school and the community of which it is a part is a phenomenon which requires a great deal of directed energy and attention. Good public relations do not just happen—they are carefully cultivated and developed.

The school principal occupies a key position in the relationship that exists between his school and the community. His major responsibility is to maintain open lines of communication between the school and its many community groups. Communication can be effected in a variety of ways, including written communication, personal conversations, press releases, attendance at meetings, involvement in community affairs, and by active teacher participation in community activities. The principal should also encourage community groups to become involved with appropriate aspects of the school program. By so doing he gains their support and aid and increases their awareness of what the school is attempting to achieve. By keeping his community well informed, the principal is greatly enriching the potential for positive public interest in education. His role in the public relations program, therefore, is an important aspect of the principal's over-all role as educational leader.

The role of the principal in the community was discussed in Chapter II. In brief, the principal has many groups which serve as major referents to him and in some way influence and direct the role he plays. This notion may seem to imply that the school principal must become what every group wants him to become. This is impossible—no man can be all things to all other men. The principal must not be merely a reactor to the pressures of groups around him, yielding to the strongest influence. Often that is the easiest, most expedient path to follow, but doing so the principal yields the leadership he should hold.

By virtue of his training, experience, and expertise, the principal must expect to be sought out by non-educators in his community as the man best qualified to give direction and leadership to the educational program. If the direction he favors is not popular, he must educate the groups around him to see the merit of his position. Where possible the principal must influence those around him to strike out in new directions. The principal must be flexible, tempering his leadership with tact and discretion. He must decide an order of priorities for points in his program.

Sometimes the principal and powerful elements in the community may take irreconcilably opposed stands, and the principal may have to leave the system. This is a step many administrators must take as the sole alternative to compromising the integrity of their beliefs.

Whatever the situation, one point is crucially clear. The school principal should be the educational leader in his community. His community must regard him in this light and must look to him for guidance in matters of education. For the principal, this is a "splendid misery" which must be borne. It is an expectation for his position which is realized only when the principal assumes the posture of a leader in education.

CHAPTER VII

Principal's Functions: Managing the School

The fourth major function of the school principal relates to his management of certain matters including student personnel, finance and business matters, plant maintenance, and auxiliary services that may be termed the *supportive* aspects of the instructional program. They are important adjuncts to the teaching-learning process and therefore require careful surveillance and attention.

In many school systems it is becoming standard practice to allocate some of the responsibility for the management of these functions to an official in the central office, usually a business director responsible to the superintendent. Be that as it may, there are many tasks related to each area which the principal himself must perform.

Student Personnel

Hencley and McCleary asked a sample of more than a hundred secondary school principals what problems involving student personnel they encountered most frequently.[1] All the problems identified by the principals were categorized and listed, in order of diminishing frequency of occurrence, as follows:

1. Discipline;
2. Providing guidance and counseling;
3. Dropouts;
4. Poor attendance;
5. Student-teacher relationships;
6. Student activities;
7. Changing enrollments: both size and composition of a student body;
8. Slow learners;
9. College admissions;
10. Pupil reporting.

The authors go on to point out that:

---

[1] Lloyd E. McCleary and Stephen P. Hencley, *Secondary School Administration: Theoretical Bases of Professional Practice* (New York: Dodd, Mead and Co., 1965), p. 249.

For the principal who wishes to solve rather than to live with the kinds of problems reported above, an appropriate beginning seems to lie in the way the program is conceived by the principal himself. He must come to see that services are needed beyond mere classroom instruction and a few student activities. Personnel services . . . must be viewed as being related—concerned with helping youth to a clearer and more certain understanding of himself and others, and of the possibilities in the situations he faces.[2]

Two related facets of student personnel services are the organization of special programs and activities for students, and the collection of appropriate data upon which sound decisions about students can be made.

Special programs and activities. "The heart of every school is the individual learner to be served by it, and he is even more basic than students in the collective sense."[3] This statement embodies the philosophy that recognizes the need for and justifies the existence of special programs and activities for a school's students. Students do not all learn at the same rate, suffer the same personal problems, or cope equally with the rigorous demands of the school program. Each student faces his world differently and he must be given whatever assistance he may need to help him live successfully in the generalized world around him. Such assistance is provided through special programs and activities sponsored by the school.

Where a school district maintains a special service program in each of its schools, the high school programs typically are far more comprehensive than those in the elementary schools. Most secondary schools have full-time guidance counselors and a nurse; some also have speech and remedial-reading specialists. Problems beyond the scope of such in-school specialists are usually referred to specialists attached to the central office, such as psychologists and social workers, or to outside community agencies.

Except in wealthier districts, program specialists are seldom assigned on a full-time basis to elementary schools. Such specialists may be attached to the central office staff, dividing their time among the several elementary schools of the district. Often the time a specialist can spend in each school is too minimal to constitute an adequate special service program. Heavy demand for the services of a limited number of specialists at the central office may sidetrack special-case referrals for a long time, and it is not uncommon that

2 *Ibid.,* p. 249.
3 John E. Corbally Jr., T. J. Jensen, and W. Frederick Staub, *Educational Administration: The Secondary School* (Boston: Allyn and Bacon Inc., 1961), p. 159.

teachers and principals in the elementary schools are substantially left to their own devices to cope with their students' problems.

What role the principal will play in providing special services depends greatly on whether or not specialists are available in his district. If they are, the principal makes his greatest contribution by bringing together specialist, teacher, and problem student (and, if it be necessary, the parents) in order that they may together work out a solution to the problem. If professional help is not available, finding solutions to his students' problems will present a great challenge to the principal's leadership. How well he copes with the situation will, in many ways, reflect the depth of his knowledge of community resources and his understanding of students.

Special programs need not be only for students with problems. Many schools have gifted students who need the challenge of new and different learning experiences. The principal must encourage his teachers to plan activities appropriate for these students that will give them outlets for their giftedness. Principals from several schools have done well to pool their efforts and resources to plan a program bringing together the gifted children from all the schools. The principal must be cognizant that students of high potential require special programs, and that it is his responsibility to see they are provided.

One other aspect of special programs concerns the extracurricular activities of the school. Such activities as interscholastic athletics, intramural activities, student publications, dramatics, and special interest groups such as clubs are all properly a part of the extra-curriculum of the school. Important adjuncts to the total school program though they be, the principal must take care to see that they are not overextended. A proper balance within the total program consistent with the rationale of the total educational enterprise must be maintained.

Data collection. The other facet of pupil personnel services concerns the collection of relevant data which are useful in making decisions about each student.[4] Data on school census, attendance, home environments, achievement in school, standardized test results and the like are useful in making decisions affecting classification of students by grade, student promotion, scheduling of programs, and the like.

---

[4] For a comprehensive discussion of this topic see Paul B. Jacobson, William C. Reavis, and James D. Logsden, *The Effective School Principal* (Englewood Cliffs, N.J.: Prentice-Hall, Inc. 1963), pp. 379–403; also see Stephen J. Knezevich, *Administration of Public Education* (New York: Harper & Brothers, 1962), Chapter 11.

It is the principal's responsibility to see that relevant data are collected and kept up to date. He must also insure that these data are used by the people in his school who should be using them. By making records easily accessible, and by encouraging his professional staff to use them, the principal develops the concept that the data are useful tools in decision-making about each student.

Finance and Business

Contemporary educational programs entail expenditure of great sums of money.[5] Funds must be raised, and machinery for the control of and accounting for expenditures must be established to insure that money is being spent wisely. In many school districts, the major responsibility for overseeing the expenditure of funds is vested with a business manager. School principals are involved in this task, but the degree of involvement varies considerably among school districts.

Often a principal is asked by the superintendent to prepare a statement of his school's upcoming fiscal needs. Such statements are prepared after the principal and his staff have reviewed the adequacy of available resources and materials to meet the objectives of the school program. Where possible, funds are appropriated in accordance with a school's need.

It is incumbent upon the principal to establish and maintain accepted procedures for accounting appropriations received and funds expended. In this regard Hencley and McCleary make the following recommendations:

1. All money received should be traceable through official receipts.
2. All cash receipts should be banked.
3. Individuals responsible for the final safekeeping of school funds should be bonded.
4. All disbursements should be by check except for small purchases made from petty cash.
5. Official documents (such as requisition forms, memorandum accounts, receipts, canceled checks, and check vouchers) should be on file and accessible for inspection.
6. The records should permit preparation of monthly bank reconciliation statements.

---

[5] For a comprehensive discussion of the financing of public education in the United States see Paul R. Mort, Walter C. Reusser, and John W. Polley, *Public School Finance*, 3d. ed. (New York: McGraw-Hill Book Company, Inc., 1960).

7. Financial statements encompassing all transactions should be prepared monthly and yearly.

8. Copies of yearly audit statements should be placed on file in the school district's central office.[6]

In some schools, especially at the secondary level, funds are raised through student activities involving ticket sales for athletic and dramatic events, club dues, bookstore sales, and special projects. Monitoring the expenditure of such funds is the principal's responsibility. In this regard McCleary and Hencley suggest the following guidelines:

1. The principal should assume responsibility for developing policies to guide fund-raising and fund-disbursing activities.

2. Control procedures in the school's accounting system should encompass all fund-raising and fund-disbursing transactions associated with extra curricular activities.

3. Transfer of funds from one account to another should be carefully regulated.

4. The general school fund should not become the vehicle for providing equipment and purchases which are the responsibility of the board of education.[7]

In summary, the school principal in many cases will have responsibility for expending certain funds, and he should adopt measures to insure that full value will be received for them.

School plant maintenance. The school plant may be viewed as the physical expression of an education program. Each component of the school plant—classrooms, offices, work centers, health and guidance rooms, library, lunchroom, auditorium, and so on—should be considered in relation to its educational functions and to the persons it is expected to serve. The principal should be familiar with the features of each component and the maximum potential each has as an educational area. Together with teachers, custodians, and others of his staff, the principal must study the plant carefully to determine the most efficient means for using each component of it. Through the collection and careful examination of relevant data it may be found, for example, that certain rooms are being underutilized or are being utilized incorrectly. Incorrect usage of a room can impose unnecessary limitations on the school program.

Several criteria for evaluating the school plant have been suggested by the American Association of School Administrators.[8]

---

[6] Lloyd E. McCleary and Stephen P. Hencley, *op. cit.*, p. 324.

[7] *Ibid.*, p. 330.

[8] American Association of School Administrators, *American School Buildings* (Washington, D.C.: The Association, 1949), p. 8.

These criteria are:

1. Curriculum Adequacy: Does the building provide the space and facilities for the educational program needed by the community for its children, youth, and adults?

2. Safety and Wellbeing: Does the building protect against danger and provide a positive influence for improving the health and physical welfare of the pupils?

3. Interfunctional Coordination: Is the facility so planned that the activity in each part of the building may be coordinated harmoniously with related activities and may be carried on effectively without disturbing other activities?

4. Efficiency and Utility: Is the facility so planned that the handling of materials and the comings and goings of pupils, school staff and the public are accomplished with a minimum of interference and a maximum of ease and satisfaction to all concerned?

5. Beauty: Is the facility pleasing in appearance, with simplicity, usefulness and balance as ideals, rather than ornamentation and symmetry?

6. Adaptability: Is the facility so planned that it can be enlarged or rearranged internally to meet new educational demands with a minimum of additional cost?

7. Economy: Is the facility so planned that in original outlay and in future operation the utmost in educational utility can be secured for every dollar spent?

Many of these criteria are applied when blueprints for a new building are being drawn, an activity in which—ideally—the principal will be involved and his advice and that of teachers will be sought.[9] The criteria may be used however, to assess the merits of an existing plant.

Managing custodians. Any principal will agree it is essential to have a good custodial staff. Custodial personnel who work congenially with the staff and students, who maintain high standards of care and cleanliness, and who function with minimal interference of regular activities are crucial to the effective operation of the school program. The principal has the responsibility of supervising the work of the custodians and of establishing effective custodial-professional staff relations.

Auxiliary Services

Auxiliary services include such services as cafeteria, library, health, and pupil transportation. Because they are important ad-

---

[9] For a comprehensive account of planning a school plant see Wallace H. Strevell and Arvid J. Burke, *Administration of the School Building Program* (New York: McGraw-Hill Book Company, Inc., 1959).

juncts to the on-going program of instruction, these services are important areas of concern for the school principal.[10]

Cafeteria services. Cafeteria service has become one of the most important of auxiliary school services, owing in large measure to government-supported school lunch programs. Today, it is not uncommon to find that the entire student enrollment in many schools in the country is given the opportunity to participate in this federally supported school lunch program. It is the responsibility of the principal to govern student use of the cafeteria. He must schedule and provide for the supervision of student lunch periods.

There are a great number of tasks involved with the management of cafeteria services, of which the few following are illustrative:

1. Providing sufficient numbers of serving personnel to move six to eight pupils per minute through every point in each service line.
2. Coordinating the serving rate established by service lines with the seating capacity of the eating areas.
3. Making sure that kitchen facilities and service equipment will permit fulfillment of established service goals.
4. Directing concerted effort toward reduction of noise and odors.
5. Establishing desired standards of student conduct.
6. Making sure that health standards in relation to food cleanliness, balanced diets, and general sanitation are of a high order and serve as examples from which students may learn and profit.
7. Creating official avenues such as faculty and student committees for channeling suggestions concerning menu improvement, service standards, pupil conduct, and other matters of concern to cafeteria patrons, cafeteria personnel, and administrative officers.[11]

As may be seen, the management of cafeteria services can demand a great deal of the principal's time and energy. In most cases, he is provided with assistants to whom he can delegate certain of these tasks; the extent of his own involvement with cafeteria services will vary with the number and effectiveness of those assistants.

Library services. More and more the school library is coming to be viewed as an important, integral part of the school program. As instructional programs become more complex and demanding, students find themselves forced to augment information derived from textbooks with other resource books and materials. The principal has the responsibility of developing the library by arranging for provision of resources and personnel and by encouraging stu-

---

[10] For a discussion of auxiliary services see Lloyd E. McCleary and Stephen Hencley, *op. cit.,* pp. 335–352. These authors include school plant maintenance as part of auxiliary services. In this section, school plant is treated separately.
[11] *Ibid.,* p. 340.

dents to use these. If a librarian is on his staff, the principal must supervise her work and integrate her contribution with the total educational program. In the absence of a librarian the principal must help teachers operate the library in a manner that will make use of the library a meaningful experience to all concerned.

Transportation services. The expansion of educational opportunities for all students, coupled with the increased distances that students must travel in order to avail themselves of these opportunities, have made it necessary for school districts to provide transportation for students at all levels. In many states, the distance beyond which students must be provided with school transportation is prescribed by statute.

In school districts that provide student transportation, transportation practices and procedures are usually governed by a system-wide policy. Because it affects students in every school, the district's principals should be involved in setting the district's transportation policy.

The implementation of school transportation policy is a direct concern of the school principal. He must be involved with such matters as setting transportation schedules, regulating and supervising the work of bus drivers, informing parents of rules and regulations, and developing procedures to insure the safety of all concerned. He must also see that records are maintained in order that complete reports on all aspects of the transportation services can be made.

Health services. The promotion of sound physical wellbeing and good health habits should be a vital part of the school program. In many school districts, medical and dental services are provided either through the school system itself or through a community agency. In some school districts school nurses are assigned to serve the health needs of the student. It is the principal's responsibility to see that the professional health service offered in his school is properly utilized. This suggests that he must establish good relationships between the instructional staff and the health staff in such a way that each complements the efforts of the other.

The Principal and School Management

The myriad activities in managing a school can prove discouraging to a principal ill-equipped to handle them. Indeed there is research evidence which points to a negative relationship between a principal's self-evaluation of his administrative skills and his Executive Performance Leadership.[12] The implication seems to be that the less the principal's concern about his management duties the greater his opportunity to provide leadership to his staff. The view can be taken that the managerial functions consume time and energy at the expense of leadership activities which the principal feels he would like to perform but from which involvement in managerial activities hold him back.

This view is short-sighted. As Hemphill and others point out, "administrative performance is much more than leadership and . . . when leadership is stressed to the exclusion of other aspects of administration, an incomplete picture is presented."[13] Success in the performance of many managerial tasks is extremely vital to the success of the on-going school program. Teachers need supplies and materials, the building must be cared for, special service programs must be maintained, and many, many other tasks that, adjuncts to the program though they be, must nonetheless be carried out. If a principal is overwhelmed by his tasks, it might be that with a rescheduling of his time and given the aid of an assistant he could be released from some things the better to accomplish others. He must realize however, that his successful accomplishment of the managerial aspects of the total school program is necessary to the success of this program. His role as principal encompasses these functions; he cannot abandon them.

---

[12] Neal Gross and Robert E. Herriott, *The Professional Leadership of Elementary School Principals* (Washington, D.C.: The Cooperative Research Branch, Project No. 853, U.S. Office of Education, April 1964), Chapter 8, p. 6. The administrative skills referred to here include keeping the school office running smoothly, general planning for the school, directing the work of administrative assistants, cutting red tape when fast action is needed, publicizing the work of the school.

[13] John K. Hemphill, *et al., Administrative Performance and Personality* (New York: Bureau of Publications, Teachers' College, Columbia University, 1962), p. 345.

CHAPTER VIII

Leadership Behavior of School Principals

In his position as designated head of a school, the principal can exercise the authority and power formally vested in the office of the principalship.[1] His designation as their principal does not necessarily make the incumbent the real leader of the school's professional staff, however, as Griffiths points out:

> Although the principal . . . is the appointed head of the school, the staff may well have a member who exercises more control over the teachers than does the principal. In faculty meetings, the ideas of this individual have more weight than the principal's. He is also sought out by teachers when they want advice. He really exercises "important positive influence acts" on the teachers because they want him to.[2]

Despite the fact that the principal is the designated head of the school, then, he may or may not at the same time be the leader of the staff. Thus it may be said that granting leaders are found among school principals, not all principals can be called leaders.

Definition of Leadership

The important distinction between *leadership* and *headship* lies in the ability of the leader to "engage in acts that initiate a structure-in-interaction as part of the process of solving a mutual problem."[3] The principal performs a leadership act when he influences others in a certain direction as they seek solutions to mutual problems. These "others" include teachers, custodians, clerks, pupils, parents,

---

[1] For a discussion of headship positions see Cecil A. Gibb, "The Principals and Traits of Leadership," *Journal of Abnormal and Social Psychology,* Vol. 42 (July 1947), 267–284.

[2] Daniel E. Griffiths, *Human Relations in School Administration* (New York: Appleton-Century-Crofts, Inc., 1956), p. 236.

[3] John K. Hemphill "Administration as Problem-Solving," in *Administrative Theory in Education,* Andrew W. Halpin, ed. (Chicago: Midwest Administration Center, University of Chicago, 1958), p. 98. Hemphill defines structure-in-interaction as "a consistency in behavior occurring during interaction that permits the prediction of the behavior that will occur in future interaction" (*ibid., p. 96*).

citizens—in fine, anyone who could be considered a referent for the principalship.

This view of leadership is useful in overcoming some of the barriers to understanding the principalship that were mentioned in Chapter I. As more principals adopt the posture of leadership as it is thus defined, they will draw closer in mutuality of interests and outlook. Such mutuality could lead to a decreased emphasis on the differences between elementary and secondary school principals and could culminate in a unified, research-based literature on the generic principalship.

Research in Leadership

The research on leadership has followed several approaches. An early focus was upon sets of personality characteristics or traits which were supposed to differentiate leaders from followers. The assumption behind this approach was that successful leadership behavior was a function of the unique personality structure of an individual. Studies based upon this assumption were weakened for want of universally accepted criteria of leadership success and of precise measuring devices. Gouldner reviewed the literature in leadership and concluded that "at this time there is no reliable evidence concerning the existence of universal leadership traits."[4]

Stogdill, in a review of the literature on traits imputed to leaders, suggested that "the qualities, characteristics, and skills required in a leader are determined to a large extent by the demands of the situation in which he is to function as a leader."[5] This view represents a second approach to the study of leadership. Under the assumption that every situation requires leadership behavior that is unique to it, studies were conducted to discover the significant leadership characteristics within a particular situation.

A third approach to the study of leadership is based upon the assumption that situations are not all unique, that rather there is a certain commonality among them. In this approach, administration is viewed as a social process which requires differing styles of leadership under certain circumstances.[6] Studies using social system

---

[4] Alvin W. Gouldner, ed., *Studies in Leadership* (New York: Harper & Bros., 1950), p. 34.

[5] Ralph M. Stogdill, "Personal Factors Associated with Leadership: A Survey of the Literature," in *Journal of Psychology*, Vol. 25 (January 1948), 63.

[6] Jacob W. Getzels and Egon G. Guba, "Social Behavior and the Administrative Process," *School Review* 65 (Winter 1957), 423–41.

analysis were conducted to examine leadership behavior in differing institutions.

In varying degrees, studies of the school principal have tended to reflect all of these approaches.

Leadership Traits of the School Principal

Several studies have been undertaken to examine the relationship between the personal traits of the school principal and the perceptions of his effectiveness or success on the job. These studies provide data which suggest that there are certain traits which tend to be related to successful performance in the principalship.

Lipham studied 84 principals from all levels of education to determine the relationship between certain personal variables and effective behavior in the school principal's role.[7] He found that the personal conduct of the effective school principal was different from that of the ineffective principal.

> Composite results of the assessment procedures portrayed the effective principal as inclined to engage in strong and purposeful activity, concerned with achieving success and positions of higher status, able to relate well to others, secure in interpersonal relationships and stable in the face of highly effective stimuli. The ineffective principal was described as deliberate and preoccupied with speculative reasoning, accepting with a meek and servile attitude his present level of achievement and status, lacking the skills essential for working with adults but anxious to give assistance and consolation to children, highly dependent upon others for support and likely to exhibit strong emotional reactions in upsetting situations.[8]

Savage and Beem analyzed the findings of a study by Sternloff[9] and concluded that:

> The successful administrator is distinguished from the unsuccessful by the kind of judgement he exercises, his ethical and moral standards, his grasp or knowledge of human behavior, his emotional stability, his skills in interpersonal relationships and other personal characteristics, such as courage.[10]

---

[7] James M. Lipham, "Personal Variables Related to Administrative Effectiveness" (Doctoral dissertation, Department of Education, University of Chicago, 1960).

[8] James M. Lipham, "Personal Variables of Effective Administrators," in *Administrator's Notebook,* Vol. IX, No. 1 (September 1960).

[9] Robert E. Sternloff, "The Critical Requirements for School Administrators Based Upon an Analysis of Critical Incidents" (Doctoral dissertation, School of Education, University of Wisconsin, 1953).

[10] William W. Savage and Harlen D. Beem, "The Effective Administrator," in *Administrator's Notebook,* Vol. II, No. 2 (October 1953).

Prince suggests that the personal values held by a principal play an important role in how others view him. His study indicates that value differences between teachers and principals affect the teacher's confidence in the principal's leadership and the teacher's rating of the principal's effectiveness.[11]

Campbell studied teacher-principal agreement on teacher role and found that:

> The highly satisfied teachers consistently referred to certain attributes of their principals, such as, scholarly attitude, general competency, making the teacher feel worthy, guidance without interference, making it easy for teachers to teach, maintaining good discipline, patience, understanding, fine personality and courteous manner.[12]

Gross and Herriott attempted to relate the elementary school principal's social skills to his Executive Performance Leadership.[13] The principal's teachers and supervisors were asked to rate him as *outstanding, excellent, good, fair, poor,* or *very poor* on his leadership in:

1. Resolving student discipline problems;
2. Handling parental complaints;
3. Handling delicate interpersonal situations;
4. Obtaining parental cooperation with the school;
5. Developing *esprit de corps* among teachers.[14]

Insofar as these items may be used to define the concept, the researchers concluded that the greater a principal's social skills, the greater his Executive Performance Leadership score.

Hemphill and associates carried on an exhaustive study of the behavior of 232 elementary school principals in a simulated school setting.[15] The researchers were able to isolate eight first-order factors (Exchanging Information; Discussing Before Acting; Complying With Suggestions; Analyzing the Situation; Maintaining Organ-

---

[11] Richard Prince, "Individual Values and Administrative Effectiveness," in *Administrator's Notebook,* Vol. II, No. 2 (October 1953).

[12] Merton V. Campbell, "Teacher-Principal Agreement on the Teacher Role," in *Administrator's Notebook,* Vol. 7, No. 6 (February 1959).

[13] Neal Gross and Robert E. Herriott, *The Professional Leadership of Elementary School Principals* (Washington, D.C.: Cooperative Research Branch, U.S. Office of Education, Contract No. 853, April 1964).

[14] *Ibid.,* Chap. 8, pp. 24–25.

[15] John K. Hemphill, Daniel E. Griffiths and Norman Frederiksen, *Administrative Performance and Personality* (New York: Bureau of Publications, Teachers College, Columbia University, 1962).

izational Relationships; Organizing Work; Responding to Outsiders; Directing the Work of Others) and two second-order factors (Preparations for Decision; Amount of Work). These factors, called by the researchers "the components of administrative performance in the elementary school principalship,"[16] were found to be related to certain personal traits including abilities and knowledge, personality, interest and values, and professional concerns.[17] The authors point out:

> One of the more striking findings of the study is the appearance of many orderly relationships between personality factors and performance of the principals in the complex situations in Whitman School. Such findings were somewhat unexpected in view of the general difficulty of demonstrating relationships between measures of personality variables and job performance which has characterized much past research. Although intuitively it seems necessary that variations in personality should be expressed in job performance, progress toward achieving understanding in this area has been meager. The lack of progress may be due, in part, to the methodological problems which this study has made somewhat clearer.[18]

Pierce and Merrill reviewed research on traits and attributes that influence leader behavior and concluded:

> Traits and attributes which may be considered as bearing positive relationships to leader behavior of a significant character are popularity, originality, adaptability, judgment, ambition, persistence, emotional stability, social and economic status, and communicative skills. The highest correlations with leader behavior were found to be popularity, originality, and judgment.
> Traits that are considered to be of some significance, but not on the basis of statistical treatment, are insight, initiative, and cooperation.
> Traits and attributes that may be considered to be positively related to leader behavior, but with low statistical correlation, are disposition, responsibility, integrity, self-confidence, social activity and mobility, social skills, physical characteristics and fluency of speech.
> Conflicting findings were reported with respect to the relationship of leader behavior to dominance and extroversion-introversion.[19]

---

16 *Ibid.*, p. 342.
17 *Ibid.*, pp. 328–329.
18 *Ibid.*, p. 356.
19 Truman M. Pierce and E. C. Merrill Jr., "The Individual and Administrative Behavior," in *Administrative Behavior in Education*, R. F. Campbell and R. T. Gregg, eds. (New York: Harper & Bros., 1957), p. 331.

The authors point out that a successful leader should possess at least several of the traits in some combination.[20]

Dimensions of Leadership Style

Research evidence indicates that traits represent but one aspect of leadership. Of great importance also is the setting within which the leader's role is performed. The current view of leadership highlights two related but conceptually different dimensions of organization:

1. The organizational tasks which must be accomplished;
2. The satisfaction of the personal needs of individuals who work in the organization.

The leader's responsibility is to maintain these dimensions in dynamic equilibrium while maximizing the potential for each.[21] His ability to do this is a function of his leadership style.

Studies on leadership carried out at Ohio State University led to the development of an instrument known as the *Leadership Behavior Description Questionnaire* (LBDQ), by which two major dimensions of leadership behavior may be measured.[22] These dimensions are (1) *Consideration,* which refers to behavior that reflects friendship, mutual trust, respect, and warmth in the relationship between the leader of a group and its members; and (2) *Initiating Structure-in-Interaction,* which refers to the leader's behavior in delineating the relationship between himself and the members of his group and in endeavoring to establish well-defined patterns of organization, channels of communication, and ways of getting a job done.[23] The two dimensions, referred to here as Consideration (C) and Initiating Structure (S), offer a useful way of viewing leadership behavior when organized into a quadrant scheme.[24]

---

[20] *Ibid.,* p. 332.

[21] For a discussion of this concept, see Richard C. Lonsdale "Maintaining the Organization in Dynamic Equilibrium," in *Behavioral Science and Educational Administration,* Sixty-third Yearbook of the National Society for the Study of Education, Daniel E. Griffiths, ed. (Chicago: University of Chicago Press, 1964), pp. 142–177.

[22] Andrew W. Halpin and B. James Winer, "A Factorial Study of the Leader Behavior Descriptions," in *Leader Behavior: Its Description and Measurement,* Ralph M. Stogdill and Alvin E. Coons, eds. (Columbus: Bureau of Business Research, Ohio State University, 1957), pp. 39–51.

[23] Andrew W. Halpin, "The Superintendent's Effectiveness as a Leader," in *Administrator's Notebook,* Vol. VII, No. 2 (October 1958).

[24] Adapted from Halpin, *ibid.*

I N S I T T R I U A C T T I U N R G E		
	-C +S (1)	+C +S (2)
	-C -S (3)	+C -S (4)

CONSIDERATION

According to this scheme a principal's leadership style may reflect any one of the following combinations:

1. Low Consideration ($-$C) and High Initiating Structure ($+$S)
2. High Consideration ($+$C) and High Initiating Structure ($+$S)
3. Low Consideration ($-$C) and Low Initiating Structure ($-$S)
4. High Consideration ($+$C) and Low Initiating Structure ($-$S)

Using the LBDQ, Evenson conducted a study of perceptions of the leadership behavior of 40 high school principals.[25] He found among other things that:

1. Teachers do not agree with either their principal or their superintendent in their perceptions of the principal's behavior on the Consideration dimension. The teachers' perceptions were significantly lower than the superintendent's perception on both dimensions and significantly lower than the principals' perceptions on Consideration.

2. In general, the principal does not see himself as does his staff or his superintendent in respect to either Consideration or Initiating Structure.

3. The superintendents when compared with staff members, tend to describe principals as higher on both Consideration and Initiating Structure; the superintendents do not differ significantly from the principal in this respect.

4. Whereas only 13 principals (of the 40) are described by their teaching staffs as being both high in Consideration and high in Initiating Structure, 37 of the 40 staffs believed that these dimensions characterize the leadership behavior of an ideal principal. Conversely, though 12 of the principals are described as low in Consideration and low in Initiating Structure, the staffs unanimously agreed that an ideal principal would not behave in this fashion.

The LBDQ provides one means for examining the leadership be-

[25] Warren L. Evenson, "The Leadership Behavior of High School Principals' Perceptions and Expectations of Superintendents, Principals and Staff Members" (Doctoral dissertation, Department of Education, University of Chicago, 1958).

havior or style of the school principal. More research relating this instrument to such factors as effectiveness, personality characteristics and the like is needed for a better understanding of this form of leadership style.

Another form of leadership style is suggested by Getzels and Guba, who view administration as a social process.[26] The school may be viewed as a social system which brings together the need for task achievement (the nomothetic dimension) with the need for personal fulfillment (idiographic dimension). The model may be depicted schematically as follows:

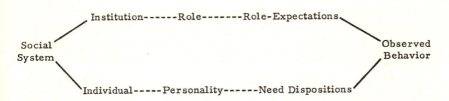

Nomothetic Dimension

Institution------Role-------Role-Expectations

Social System

Observed Behavior

Individual-----Personality------Need Dispositions

Idiographic Dimension

Basically this model suggests that the behavior of an individual in the social system (in this case the school) is related to his ability to meet the role expectations set for him in a manner which is consistent with his own needs and desires.[27]

This model has proved useful in guiding studies which have shown that a relationship exists between role expectations, need dispositions, and satisfaction in teaching, as well as effectiveness and confidence in leadership.[28]

The model also suggests three leadership styles which Moser has defined as follows:

1. The nomothetic style is characterized by behavior which stresses goal accomplishment, rules and regulations and centralized

[26] Jacob W. Getzels and Egon G. Guba, "Social Behavior and the Administrative Process," in *School Review* 65 (Winter 1957), 423–41.

[27] For a discussion of this topic, see "A New Concept of Staff Relations," *Administrator's Notebook,* Vol. VIII, No. 7 (March 1960).

[28] For example, see Merton V. Campbell, "Self-Role Conflict Among Teachers and its Relationship to Satisfaction Effectiveness and Confidence in Leadership" (Doctoral dissertation, Department of Education, University of Chicago, 1958); also see Donald C. Moyer, "Teachers' Attitudes toward Leadership as They Relate to Teacher Satisfaction" (Doctoral dissertation, Department of Education, University of Chicago, 1954).

authority at the expense of the individual. Effectiveness is rated in terms of behavior toward accomplishing the school's objectives.

2. The idiographic style is characterized by behavior which stresses the individuality of people, minimum rules and regulations, decentralized authority and highly individualistic relationships with subordinates. The primary objective is to keep subordinates happy and contented.

3. The transactional style is characterized by behavior which stresses goal accomplishment but which also makes provision for individual need fulfillment. The transactional leader balances nomothetic and idiographic behavior and thus judiciously utilizes each style as the occasion demands.[29]

The social systems model can prove a very useful guide to understanding the behavior of school principals. It places into sharp focus the interlocking nature of institutional expectations for goal achievement and the idiosyncratic needs of an individual who works for the institution. The implications for the behavior of the school principal are clearly pointed out by Guba:

The unique task of the administrator can now be understood as that of mediating between these two sets of behavior-eliciting forces, that is the nomothetic and the idiographic, so as to produce behavior which is at once organizationally useful as well as individually satisfying. Action which will lead to such behavior on the part of personnel is the highest expression of the administrator's act.[30]

In summary, the research on leadership suggests the following implications for the leadership role of the school principal:

1. There are certain personality traits which seem to be related to success in leadership. These traits include ambition, ability to relate well to others, emotional stability, communicative skill, and judgment. The evidence which links personality and effectiveness in leadership is far from complete and more research is needed in this area. The findings to date, however, seem to indicate that the school principal who exhibits certain of these traits has a greater potential for success in leadership than does the principal who does not exhibit such traits.

2. The principal must have a clear understanding of the goals of the institution. This does not mean that there is a fixed set of goals for the institution which the principal must strive to achieve. It does

[29] Robert F. Moser, "The Leadership Patterns of School Superintendents and School Principals," in *Administrator's Notebook,* Vol. VI, No. 1 (September 1957).

[30] Egon G. Guba, "Research in Internal Administration—What Do We Know?" in *Administrative Theory as a Guide to Action,* Roald F. Campbell and James M. Lipham, eds. (Chicago: Midwest Administration Center, University of Chicago, 1960).

suggest however, that the principal must have a sense of direction for the institution he leads. This sense of direction should be within the broad framework of the goals and objectives of the school district of which he is a member and should be consonant with the needs of the community he serves. Without such a direction the principal is unable to provide leadership which is rational, consistent, and meaningful to those who work with him.

3. To be effective in eliciting the cooperation of his staff, the principal must have an understanding of the personal and professional needs of all who work with him. The principal who is insensitive to the needs which are unique to each individual will find it difficult to understand why certain members of his staff behave as they do. Without such an understanding, and without some strategies for coping with individual differences, the principal will find it difficult to assist each member of his staff to achieve his highest professional potential.

4. Finally, the principal must be able to place into some meaningful perspective the organizational goals of the institution, the unique personal needs of each staff member, and his own personality traits. He must work to establish a climate within which all three can mesh together into some productive entity. The variations in the leadership provided by principals are, in large measure, a function of the climate which each principal is able to mold.

Leadership and Change

In recent years there has developed a view which differentiates administration from leadership. Lipham, for example, using concepts from Hemphill, defines leadership "as the initiation of a new structure or procedure for accomplishing an organization's goals and objectives and for changing an organization's goals and objectives."[31] By contrast, he defines administration as the maintenance of the current structure.[32] Thus a leader is one who innovates, one who works to initiate change in the existing order while an administrator is viewed as a stabilizing force who works to maintain the established structure.

Change in the schools. Perhaps the most striking characteristic of the twentieth century has been the tremendous burst in the production of knowledge. More is known about phenomena and of working with them than ever before. In the wake of such knowledge the need for changes in society and in its institutions, especially those related to education, is evident. However, as Carlson

---

31 James M. Lipham, "Leadership and Administration," in *Behavioral Science and Educational Administration, op. cit.,* p. 122.

32 *Ibid.*

points out, "In spite of all of the current activity, it seems fair to say that there is quite widespread pessimism about the ability of public schools to make rapid and adequate adaptation to our fast-changing times."[33] Carlson goes on to suggest that there are three barriers to change in the public schools: (1) the absence of a change agent, (2) a weak knowledge base, and (3) what he calls the domestication of public schools.[34] The first barrier applies most directly to the behavior of school administrators.

The school principal can play a key role in implementing needed changes in his own school building. If he is a leader—by definition this means one who stimulates, encourages, promotes, and rewards activities that lead to needed changes—then his staff will become aware of the fact that one of the expectations for the teacher's role is that of planning and implementing necessary changes. If, on the other hand, he chooses not to lead, then there can be a greater tendency for the staff to omit planning for change as a perceived role expectation.

One of the easiest, most deceptive roles an administrator can slip into is that of bandwagon rider. Pressures from others, or simply misguided beliefs can lead an administrator to jump at every suggestion for innovation. Such an administrator cannot be considered a leader, for as Griffiths points out, "Generally the bandwagon rider leaves no lasting change as his monument, just a faculty of weary, frustrated teachers."[35] The implication of this statement is clear. Before adopting an innovation the administrator and his staff must make a careful assessment of how, if it were implemented, the innovation would affect positively the on-going program.

The innovator. Change is brought about by innovators, "the

---

[33] Richard O. Carlson, "Barriers to Change in Public Schools," in *Change Processes in the Public Schools,* Richard O. Carlson, *et al.,* eds. (Eugene, Oregon: Center for the Advanced Study of Educational Administration, University of Oregon, 1965), p. 3.

[34] *Ibid.,* pp. 4–6. Carlson defines domestication in terms of the relationship between the school and its clients. He says, "The label of domesticated organization is used to indicate that this class of organization is protected and cared for in a fashion similar to that of a domesticated animal. They are not compelled to attend to all of the ordinary and usual needs of an organization. For example, they do not compete with other organizations for clients; in fact, a steady flow of clients is assured. There is no struggle for survival for this type of organization—existence is guaranteed" (*ibid.,* p. 6).

[35] Daniel E. Griffiths, *Leadership for Educational Change* (Albany, N.Y.: Council for Administrative Leadership, March 1965).

first members of a social system to adopt new ideas."[36] Rogers posits some generalizations on characteristics of innovators:

1. Innovators generally are young. (Research studies on farmers provide actual evidence that innovators are younger than their peers who are later adopters.)
2. Innovators have relatively high social status, in terms of amount of education, prestige ratings, and income.
3. Impersonal and cosmopolite sources of information are important to innovators. (. . . innovative industrial firms were more likely to seek new ideas from university researchers.)
4. Innovators are cosmopolite. (. . . teachers at more innovative schools usually acquired new educational ideas from outside their community.)
5. Innovators exert opinion leadership. (. . . in communities where the norms were traditional, innovators were not looked to by their peers as sources of information and advice.)
6. Innovators are likely to be viewed as deviants by their peers and by themselves. (Research studies show that farmers who innovate are perceived as deviants from the norms of the social system.)[37]

These generalizations seem to point to the innovator as being someone who is *different* from most people. He is a person with an idea, and the courage and creative knowhow to do something with it. The innovator is the person with a vision of tomorrow rather than a reverie of yesterday.

It is erroneous to expect that the principal should be the only innovator in the school. Many in the school have the potential for innovative behavior provided they are given the appropriate encouragement and support. In many ways the school principal makes one of his most important contributions to change by providing such support and encouragement.

The Principal: Administrator and Leader

It is important to point out that the role of leader and the role of administrator need not necessarily be mutually exclusive. Indeed, insofar as the principalship is concerned, both roles are quite compatible and complementary. Both must be enacted if the school is to be a forward-looking yet stable element in the community.

[36] Everett M. Rogers, "What are Innovators Like?" in *Change Processes in the Public Schools, op. cit.*, p. 55.
[37] *Ibid.*, pp. 58–59.

In his role as administrator, the principal works with his staff to preserve and transmit to present and future generations the accumulated heritage of the past. This tends to provide a certain stability to the on-going activities of the school. By lending stability to the program, the principal can instill a feeling of security and trust in those who work with him. By resisting impulsive action on hastily conceived "instant change" the principal can contribute to diminishing the feelings of insecurity among staff members and in this way obviate a major cause of intrenched resistance to change.

In order to establish his role as leader, the principal must work to develop an environment or climate which is supportive of suggestions for change and which welcomes sound and necessary innovations as important ingredients of a viable school program. The search for knowledge and for better techniques of teaching should be as integral a part of the school program as any other part of it. The concept of change should be part of the concept of education. As Gallaher points out:

> Change is a natural and inevitable consequence of the socio-cultural and physical worlds within which our collective lives are acted out and it should be as natural and just as inevitable that we should give some attention to managing the direction of that change.[38]

Teachers are more receptive to the need for change when they adopt as their *modus operandi* the notion that the forward move of education is as inevitable as the unalterable march of history. It is the principal's responsibility as leader of the organization to plant and develop such a notion.

---

[38] Art Gallaher Jr., "Directed Change in Formal Organizations," in *Change Processes in the Public Schools, op. cit.,* p. 51.

CHAPTER IX

Preparation for the Principalship

It is clear from preceding chapters that a variety of important tasks challenge today's school principal, ranging from the execution of simple managerial duties to the performance of leadership acts, the consequences of which hold important implications for the education hence the lives of many people. The complexity inherent in today's principalship is summarized and underscored by Drucker:

> I know of no job that has so many publics to satisfy, so many bosses to answer to. There is the superintendent and the school board and behind them the local governments, and the voters and the taxpayers. There is the community at large with its interest in the schools—informed or otherwise. There is the faculty and the nonprofessional staff. And of course, there are the youngsters for whose benefit all this supposedly is going on.
>
> I know of no job, moreover, that has so many different if not conflicting demands made on it. The school administrator is expected to be an educational leader and a leader in his community. But he is also expected to be a manager, working out budgets and staying within them, hiring, placing and managing people, both faculty and staff, bringing the parents close to the school—but not so close that they can interfere; and, satisfying a host of professional bodies, each with a different idea of what, the school administrator's job should be and how it should be appraised. To an outsider like myself, who is more used to the comparative simplicity of the job of the executive and administrator in business or in government, this appears an almost impossible assignment in its complexity, in the demands it has to satisfy and in the groups, interests and constituents, each of whom consider the school "their" school and the school administrator their representative and agent.[1]

How does one prepare to cope with this complexity? What learnings and competencies are necessary for effective performance as a school principal?

The answers to these and other related questions are extremely difficult to formulate with any degree of accuracy because, to date, there is no measurable, foolproof way of predicting whether or not

---

[1] Peter F. Drucker, "The Effective Administrator," *The Bulletin of the National Association of Secondary-School Principals,* Vol. 48, No. 29 (April 1964), 157.

a given administrator will be effective in his job. As was pointed out in Chapter VIII, there is some evidence to suggest that certain personality traits and behavioral acts tend to be related more to successful rather than to unsuccessful performance on the job.[2] However, the evidence is limited and inconclusive; at best it provides only a small step in the development of an ample knowledge based upon which decisions may be made regarding preparation for administrative positions in education. As a result, no preparation formula can be prescribed for an individual who wishes to become a school principal. Current knowledge can only suggest the nature of the demands upon this position and some of the more essential ingredients of a program through which one might prepare to meet these demands.

The Social Setting

One of the most critical factors influencing the demands upon the school principal is concerned with the social setting within which he operates. This setting in large measure influences the scope and the effectiveness of the principal's activities, and in this regard holds important implications for preparation for the principalship.

There are at least two important foci with regard to the social setting within which the principalship role is played. These are related to the phenomena which characterize (1) the American social scene in general and (2) the social setting of the local school district. Both are functionally bound but analytically can yield different perspectives.

The American social scene. Few people will deny that American society in the twentieth century is the most scientifically advanced in the history of man. One need but point to the many developments in space exploration, industrial productivity, medicine and its related fields, and other areas to see that at no other time in its history has there been such progress in the forward movement of this nation.

This progress, however, has brought with it problems—including social upheavals among people seeking to adapt themselves to twentieth century living, and shortage of the highly skilled individuals

---

[2] One of the most comprehensive studies on the dimensions of performance of elementary school principals is reported in John K. Hemphill, Daniel E. Griffiths, and Norman Frederiksen, *Administrative Performance and Personality* (New York: Bureau of Publications, Teachers College, Columbia University 1962). See especially Fig. 5, pp. 328–329.

required to carry on the complex activities required in this economy, and the triumphs abroad of threatening international powers —that have thrown a national spotlight on education as a factor critical to their solution.

The almost unprecedented degree of private, state, and federal support for education in the past decade is clear evidence of the place education holds among the top-priority areas of concern in modern American society. Tremendous sums are being expended to support research and development activities in education. For example, billions of dollars have been made available through such federal programs as the National Defense Education Act, the National Science Foundation, the Elementary and Secondary Education Act of 1965, and the Economic Opportunity Act. Private agencies such as Ford, Carnegie and the Kellogg Foundations are contributing great sums of money to support a tremendous variety of activities in education.

National concern for education has also been stirred by certain writings on education, notably those by James Bryant Conant. One of Conant's books, *The Education of American Teachers*[3] has enjoyed great prominence as a result of its being on the national best sellers list for a period of time. Also the great increase in the school-age population has brought education closer to more people than at any other time.

The vigorous contemporary interest in it has made education more than a local matter. The impact of education is being felt on a much larger and broader scale than ever before, with the consequence that leadership in education has attained a position of greater societal significance. The school principal, for example, has been thrust into a key leadership position in a critical social institution. The leadership he provides for this institution can have important consequences for the continuing development of American society.

The local social setting. Despite its many advances generally, society in the United States has tended to develop at a rather uneven pace. Certain areas in the country show a social development far beyond that shown in other areas. Rural areas have not kept pace with the scientific and technological developments of this century and the people who live in these areas are behind in knowledge, skills, and social maturation. The expectations they hold for edu-

---

[3] James B. Conant, *The Education of American Teachers* (New York: McGraw-Hill Book Company, Inc. 1963).

cation differ from those held by people in more socially advanced areas. The type of educational leadership provided in a socially depressed area will differ markedly from that provided in a socially advanced area. The school principal must be well versed in these differences and must adjust his behavior to accommodate them.

Perhaps the most significant factor highlighting differences of social maturity in the United States today is concerned with social integration. The degree of integration among people of varying races, ethnic groups or socioeconomic levels, is extremely divergent in this country. This is particularly evidenced in urban and suburban areas where the main struggle for social integration is being carried on. In these areas the schools are the main arenas in which the struggle for equal opportunity is being fought. If they are to provide leadership to all who are involved in this struggle, the principals of such schools must be well prepared and well informed about the needs, desires, and aspirations of socially and ethnically differentiated groups.

The research on the relationship between local school district uniquenesses and educational leadership is extremely sparse. There is need, for example, to determine the types of administrative performance and educational leadership best suited to urban, suburban, and rural areas. Such information would be extremely useful in pairing an individual with an area. Thus, through selective placement an individual could hold a principalship for which his talents and training are best suited.

Another useful contribution which could be made through such research is related to the focus of preparation programs for school administrators. It may well be that district uniquenesses and not the elementary-secondary school dichotomy must form whatever differences may pertain to preparation for the principalship.[4] These differences, when viewed in terms of district uniqueness, will not be reflected so much in the study of administration *as* administration, they will rather be reflected in the study of people, cultures, and sociological phenomena. There is some evidence that this latter emphasis is already appearing in preparation programs for school administrators.

---

[4] See Chapter I for a discussion on "Obstacles to Viewing the Principalship."

Preparing for the Principalship

The type of role the school principal is being called upon to play in modern education necessitates that he enjoy a high level of professional competency. Historically, successful classroom teachers were selected for the principalship on the assumption that success in teaching was a predication of success in school administration. Experience over the years has shown, however, that not all successful teachers can become successful school principals. The changing demands for leadership require knowledge and competencies which go beyond those required for success in teaching.

Needed competencies. A listing of all the competencies required of school principals is, of necessity, limited by the incompleteness in knowledge of what constitutes successful administration. In truth, the total study of educational administration is still in its early stages and much yet remains to be learned. However, on the basis of what is already known about administration, education, and society, certain inferences can be drawn concerning the competencies universally needed by school administrators in the United States. Among required competencies may be included the following:

1. Understanding the teaching and learning process and being able to contribute to its development.

2. Understanding school organization and being able to lead and coordinate the activities of the highly trained professional personnel who comprise this organization.

3. Understanding the nature and the composition of the local school-community and being able to maintain satisfactory relationships between the school and its many community groups.

4. Understanding the technical aspects of school administration (e.g., school building maintenance, management functions and the like) and being able to obtain and allocate resources in an effective and efficient manner.

5. Understanding the change process and being able to bring about necessary and appropriate changes in school and society.

6. Understanding various cultures and being able to plan and implement programs which will meet the unique needs of each culture in the school.

7. Understanding and being able to use the findings of relevant research.

There is no doubt that these and other related competencies are beyond the capacities of many people. Opportunities for incompetent persons to assume important leadership positions in education should be denied through some regular process of certification. Leadership in education is too crucial an activity to be left in the hands of individuals who are ill-equipped to provide it. However, where individuals show a potential for leadership, every means should be provided to prepare them to assume positions as educational administrators.

Preservice education. One of the most important and widely accepted methods for preparing to assume the position of school principal is through graduate course-work at a university. In fact, the universities play perhaps the major role in the preservice preparation of all school administrators.

In recent years the view has developed that in certain areas there should be uniformity of preservice preparation for school administrators at all levels of education. Thus, for example, a significant part of a preservice program for the principalship can be devoted to common learnings in such areas as the behavioral and social sciences, professional education, and general concepts of administration.[5] Anywhere from 50 to 75 per cent of a preservice program can be occupied with these common areas. However, beyond this there are certain special learnings which, it is suggested, are uniquely suited for the level of the principalship for which a student is preparing. In this regard, McNally and Dean make this recommendation:

> Those preparing for elementary school administration should be required to engage in specific study of:
> 1. Basic background learning in the objectives, curriculum, methodology, and organization of elementary education in the United States;
> 2. The specific problems and characteristics of the elementary school and its community as social systems;
> 3. Knowledge and techniques important in supervision and the improvement of the instructional program;
> 4. Developmental psychology of children of elementary school age;
> 5. Psychology of elementary school subjects and methodology (e.g. the psychology of learning to read, psychology underlying integrative subject matter organization).

---

[5] For a discussion of this topic see Donald J. Leu and Herbert C. Rudman, eds., *Preparation Programs for School Administrators: Common and Specialized Learnings* (East Lansing, Mich.: College of Education, Michigan State University 1963); also see Jack Culbertson and Stephen Hencley, eds., *Preparing Administrators: New Perspectives* (Columbus, Ohio: University Council for Educational Administration, 1962).

6. Substantive knowledge involved in the administration of the elementary school program.[6]

Downey describes the special preparation for the secondary school principalship in the following manner:

... the secondary school principal must equip himself with a broad educational foundation on which to base his theories of secondary education. Such a foundation should include a well-conceived personal philosophy of secondary education as well as an appreciation for all other philosophical orientations. It should include a comprehensive concept of our social institutions and the place of the high school among these institutions. It should include an appreciation for the great cultures of the world—particularly our own—and a notion of the high school's responsibility to transmit culture from generation to generation. Finally it should include a knowledge of the needs of young adults and an idea of how the secondary school could and should meet these needs.

In brief, the prospective secondary school principal should have an opportunity to think deeply about the secondary school as well as the society and the individuals it serves. His preparation program should provide that opportunity.[7]

There is emerging some controversy regarding what constitutes the specialized aspects of a program of preparation for the principalship. For example, there are some who argue that the involvement of the school principal in instructional supervision is going to become less important as specialization in teaching becomes more complex. Erickson, for example, makes the point that:

Instructional supervision by the prinicpal seems, then, to be less and less defensible in many schools, in addition it is probably becoming less necessary. If teachers follow the pattern established by other occupational groups, they will be governed more and more by internalized norms as they acquire greater expertise and will resist the supervisory and evaluative efforts of persons whom they do not recognize as fellow experts.[8]

Already in certain school districts instructional leadership responsibilities are being delegated to specially trained instructional consultants assigned full time to a given school in the district. These

[6] Harold J. McNally and Stuart E. Dean, "The Elementary School Principal," in *Preparation Programs for School Administrators: Common and Specialized Learnings*, Leu and Rudman eds., *op. cit.*, p. 121.

[7] Lawrence W. Downey, "The Secondary School Principal," *op. cit.*, p. 132.

[8] Donald A. Erickson "Changes in the Principalship: Cause for Jubilation or Despair" *The National Elementary School Principal*, Vol. XLIV, No. 5 (April 1965), 19.

consultants work with the teachers on all aspects of the instructional program.

In schools where there are instructional consultants the principals are relegated to playing a minor role in the supervision of the instructional program. In the event that such a situation becomes more prevalent (and signs point in that direction), specialized learnings related to elementary and secondary school instructional differences will become unnecessary in preparation programs for the principalship. When this happens a new format for preparing school principals will have to be developed. There is some evidence, even now, that such a format is beginning to take shape.

An important trend which is becoming more evident in the major universities concerns the emphasis being placed upon the social sciences as a significant area of study for potential school administrators. This emphasis is based upon the view that educational administrators deal with extremely complex organizations and that success in these organizations is directly related to an individual's ability to comprehend and master these complexities. The social sciences provide the assistance for developing this ability.

Goldhammer outlines five major values the social sciences have for educational administrators:

> 1. The social sciences help the educational administrator achieve both a method for the collection of data and a systematic way of looking at things.
> 2. The social sciences can help the educational administrator acquire broad knowledge of the setting in which education and the functions of administration take place.
> 3. Through the social sciences the educational administrator can gain added understanding of the significance of the phenomena with which he deals.
> 4. The social sciences can help to improve the basis which the educational administrator has for predicting the consequences of his decisions and actions.
> 5. The social sciences can help the administrator select relevant data pertaining to the concrete situations with which he must deal and also provide him with the research tools which will enable him to analyze and interpret these data or to draw adequate and accurate inferences from them.[9]

As the need for more broadly-prepared school principals gains wider acceptance, preservice programs will include more study of

---

[9] Keith Goldhammer, *The Social Sciences and the Preparation of Educational Administrators* (Columbus, Ohio: The University Council for Educational Administration, 1963), pp. 14–18.

the social sciences.[10] Conversely, as these programs place greater stress on the study of the social sciences the school principal will be better prepared to cope with the emerging cultural and social phenomena which portend significant alterations in his role.

The internship.   The view that one learns by doing is expressed in university-sponsored preparation programs as field-laboratory experience and/or through an internship. At some point in his professional study, the student of educational administration may work for a designated period of time in a school system under the supervision of a competent school administrator and a professor from the sponsoring institution. During this period the administrative intern may become involved in a variety of useful on-the-job learning experiences.

Ideally an internship in preparation for the principalship should extend over a period of one full year. During this year the intern should have some experience in working with people at all levels of administration including the superintendent. This wide range of experiences would permit the intern to gain a feel for the general responsibilities, duties, pressures, and expectations for the many positions which comprise the organization. It would also help the intern to better understand how the principalship fits into the total organizational context.

Favor for the idea of an internship as a part of the preparatory program for educational administration is growing. The authors of the 1960 AASA Yearbook felt so strongly on the importance of an internship that they made the following declaration:

> The internship is so important that it is the *sine qua non* of a modern program of preparation of educational administrators. If an institution cannot provide internship training it should not be in the business of preparing educational administrators.[11]

The obvious intent behind this statement is to have an internship experience included in all preparation programs for educational administrators. For the principalship such an inclusion would represent a strengthening in the preparation of people who occupy this position.

---

[10] For more discussion on this topic see Lawrence W. Downey and Frederick Enns, eds., *The Social Sciences and Educational Administration* (Edmonton, Alberta, Canada: Division of Educational Administration, University of Alberta, 1963).

[11] American Association of School Administrators, *Professional Administration for America's Schools* (Washington, D.C.: 1960 Yearbook of the Association, N.E.A.), p. 82.

Certification of school principals. The first elementary and secondary school principal certificates were issued in 1911 in Pennsylvania and New Jersey.[12] Since that time the practice of certifying principals has grown to the point where currently 72 per cent of the states issue certificates for elementary school principals, 70 per cent issue certificates for secondary school principals, and 34 per cent issue general certificates which encompass a variety of administrative positions.[13] This latter figure seems to indicate an increasing tendency among the states towards certifying school principals without designating the level for which the certificate was granted. Where such general certification pertains, greater flexibility is provided for preservice programs in universities, with the result that a proliferation of courses needed for certification is avoided.

Generally, certification for the principalship implies that an individual has successfully completed one or all of the following: (1) certain designated graduate courses at an accredited institution of higher education; (2) from three to five years of teaching experience; and (3) an administrative internship or its equivalent (sometimes through an assistant principalship). There are variations in these requirements among the states, with some setting more requirements than others for certification. These variations tend to limit the scope of career movement for some principals who may wish to move from one state to another. To eliminate this limitation several states have established reciprocity of certification.

In the main, the certification for the principalship by each state represents the minimum requirements set for that position. These alone, however, need not necessarily lead to competency in the position. In actual practice more than the minima that are set are desirable. In recognition of this, there has been a growing trend towards associating preparation programs in accredited universities with the certification of school administrators in a state. In this way, an aspiring school administrator would complete a set phase of a preparation program and the sponsoring university could recommend to the state education department that this individual

---

[12] Robert B. Howsam and Edgar L. Morphet, "Certification of Educational Administrators," in *The Journal of Teacher Education,* Vol. IX, No. 1 (March 1958), 7.

[13] For more data on this subject see Robert C. Woellner and M. Aurilla Wood, *Requirements for Certification of Teachers, Counselors, Librarians, Administrators for Elementary Schools, Secondary Schools, Junior Colleges, Annual Editions* (Chicago: The University of Chicago Press, all issues).

should be certified for the particular position for which he has prepared.

Generally, the phases in a preparation program are linked to both certification and university degree requirements. It appears that as this linkage becomes stronger, certification requirements and degree requirements will become synonymous, and only those holding advanced degrees will qualify for administrative positions. This will be an important upgrading for the principalship.

Continuing professional development. A particularly appropriate truism for the school principal is that he must never stop learning. The dynamic nature of his position almost mandates his continuous search for self improvement.

It is a complete fallacy to believe that upon successful completion of a preservice program an individual requires no further study or training. Indeed, it may well be said that a preservice program marks only the beginning of preparation for a position, but a continuing education program (sometimes called an *in-service* program) is the lifeline of growth and maturation in the position. An advanced degree does not guarantee complete knowledge in any area; one never knows all there is to know about his position. He must always strive for new understandings and new knowledge about ways to improve upon his abilities. The school principal in particular must constantly strive for better insights into ways of working in complex organizations, the teaching-learning process and into the realm of human behavior. These perhaps more than anything else are the tools of the principal's trade.

There are many ways by which the school principal may continue his professional education, among them:

1. Attendance at university courses and seminars;
2. Visitation to other school districts to see and study first hand, programs which have implications for his own leadership in his school building;
3. Attendance at workshops or clinics which focus upon specific administrative problems and issues;
4. Travel throughout the United States and other countries to broaden and deepen understandings of different cultures and value orientations;
5. Reading the professional literature to keep abreast of what is happening in the profession;
6. Reading and studying in the humanities to enrich understandings of life;
7. Attendance at national and regional professional meetings to keep abreast of professional issues and problems and to maintain contact and exchange ideas with others in the profession;

8. Attendance at workshops or seminars sponsored by the local school district.

These are illustrative of some of the many ways by which the school principal may continue his professional development while he is on the job. In some school districts this growth is mandated through a statement of expectations for the principal's role. These districts are likely to sponsor workshops for principals and others within the district. Some even will pay the expense for attendance at university sponsored workshops, enrollment in graduate course work, participation in professional meetings and the like. It is also becoming more and more common for school districts to provide sabbatical leaves after six or seven years of continuous service for those who wish to pursue further advanced study. A practice which is almost universally accepted among school districts is to provide increments in salary and other benefits to encourage continued professional growth. Thus, it seems that there are ample material incentives for a school principal to continue his professional education.

There is another incentive for the school principal to grow professionally, related to his affiliation with the profession.

Relating to the Profession

There are a number of organizations within the education profession to which a principal may belong. The four organizations which probably claim the greatest membership are the American Association of School Administrators (AASA), the Association for Supervision and Curriculum Development (ASCD), the Department of Elementary School Principals (DESP), and the National Association of Secondary School Principals (NASSP).[14] The first two organizations have a large number of members representing a wide range of responsibilities in a school system. The latter two are more limited in their membership. In the main the elementary school principals belong to the DESP and the secondary school principals belong to the NASSP. Each of these associations through its bulletins and other publications and through its sponsored national and regional meetings has the potential to exert a considerable influence over the principal at the local level. Through these associations the principal is provided an opportunity for a wide variety

[14] All four organizations are affiliated with the National Education Association (NEA).

of contacts with others of similar interests and orientations. The principal stands to gain much from affiliation with these groups.

He also loses something, however, as a result of the insularity among these organizations. Separation by level tends to limit the amount of professional contact elementary and secondary school principals may have. This limited contact denies the opportunity for an exchange and sharing of thoughts and ideas on mutually significant problems.

Perhaps the future of professionalism for school principals will provide for a National Organization of School Principals whose major goal will be to foster a continuing close relationship among all school principals in the United States. In such an organization, differences attributed to organizational level will be minimized and similarities related to important problems and issues facing the principalship will be maximized. When this happens the principalship will be better prepared for the challenges which face it in the twentieth century.

Challenges to the Principalship

The rapid pace of contemporary life is casting intense new challenges into the path of school administrators. Perhaps the greatest of these lies in the determination and the enactment of a course of action which preserves the best in American tradition and lends stability to education and society, yet at the same time is responsive to the need and the press for change in both. There are strong and significant proponents for each view and the inexorable forward movement of society often brings both into direct confrontation. The resulting potential for conflict poses a dilemma and a supreme challenge to leadership in education. A brief review of some of the major problems and issues which demand resolution will illustrate the complexity of this challenge. No solutions are suggested, for none are readily available.

Integration. Since the historic 1954 Supreme Court decision (Brown *et al. vs.* Board of Education, Topeka) there has been tremendous organized pressure to integrate the public schools in the United States. The Negroes and other groups have embarked on a course of action, both violent and nonviolent, which demands the abolition of racially unbalanced public schools. The consequences of such action have led to great controversy on such matters as the efficacy of the neighborhood school, the advisability of compensatory budgeting to provide more money to raise the quality of the segregated Negro schools, and the importance of busing children across attendance area lines in order to racially balance school populations. These and other related issues divide opinion among many segments of the school community and very often it is the school administrator who becomes the target of action instituted by special interest groups.

Religion.   Although it has been dwarfed in national attention by the integration issue, the problem of religion in the public schools remains an important controversy. The Constitution of the United States clearly stipulates a separation of Church and State, yet in many public schools in the country religious exercises are carried on in some form.

In many public schools a prayer and/or a reading from the Bible form part of the exercises with which the school day begins..In many schools released time from the school day is made available for those who wish to receive religious instruction in private or church-related institutions. As with integration, community groups are divided in this matter and a great deal of support can be found both for and against "religion" in the public schools. Each group exerts pressure upon the school administrator, who must find some solution which pleases all people, complies with the law of the land, is consistent with the objectives of the school program and is compatible with his own system of values and beliefs.

Political and moral ideologies.   In addition to the preceding issues around which community interest may be generated, there are other factors which arouse certain citizens to action. Two such factors are the political and the moral ideologies by which people live. There are for example, some groups which oppose certain school programs (e.g., teaching about Communism or about the United Nations) and are able to bring considerable pressure upon school officials. Other groups form in opposition to certain literature presented as part of the school program. For example, some groups object to certain literature on the grounds that it is perceived to be pornographic or immoral. The militancy and strength of these groups is often overbearing, yet school administrators must cope with them.

Teacher militancy.   Teacher organizations have long had some influence in the operation of the schools. In recent years, however, the demand for greater influence by teachers has been expressed by the highly organized and sometimes militant American Federation of Teachers, often referred to as "the teachers union." The American Federation of Teachers has sponsored teacher strikes to obtain improved benefits and to win a greater and more significant role in policy formulation for the schools. These actions have forced new and different relationships between administrators and teachers.

Instructional supervision.   The literature on the principalship (indeed on all educational administration) is filled with exhortations and clarion calls for "leadership in education." Traditionally this has been taken to mean that the school principal must hold as his primary, all-encompassing task the improvement of instruction in his building. Inherent in this task has been the expectation that the principal must supervise his teachers to ensure that they are performing their tasks effectively. This expectation for the principal has come under serious questioning, however, on the grounds that teachers are becoming more highly specialized and require equally specialized individuals to supervise their work, and that emerging patterns of instructional practices call for a greater interdependence among teachers and other specialists and a lesser need for dominance by other administrators.[15]

Whither the Principalship?

The issues and problems which face today's school principal are not easily resolved. There is need for a careful, studied appraisal of his functions, responsibilities, and role in light of the challenges of twentieth-century society and the demands for educational leadership contained therein. As the challenges vary, so too will the demands be different for each school principal.

Perhaps the best answer to our question will be found in the "sustained dialogue between those in the world of discovery and those in the world of practice."[16] Such a dialogue, leading as it must to carefully studied action, should form the basis upon which the principalship develops further and assumes an even more prominent position in the exciting and challenging years which lie ahead for education in the United States.

---

[15] For a discussion of these and other points see Donald A. Erickson, "Forces for Change in the Principalship," in *The Elementary School Journal,* Vol. 65, No. 6 (November 1964), 57–64.

[16] Luvern L. Cunningham, "Continuing Professional Education for Elementary Principals," in *The National Elementary Principal,* Vol. XLIV, No. 5 (April 1965), 62.

Bibliography

Administrator's Notebook. Chicago: Midwest Administration Center, The University of Chicago, all issues.

Association for Supervision and Curriculum Development, *Balance in the Curriculum.* Washington, D.C.: The Association, 1961.

Callahan, Raymond C., *Education and the Cult of Efficiency.* Chicago: The University of Chicago Press, 1962.

Campbell, Roald F., John E. Corbally Jr., and John A. Ramseyer (2nd edition) *Introduction to Educational Administration.* Boston: Allyn and Bacon, Inc. 1962.

Campbell, Roald F., and Russell T. Gregg, eds., *Administrative Behavior in Education.* New York: Harper & Bros. 1957.

Campbell, Roald F., and John A. Ramseyer, *The Dynamics of School-Community Relationships.* Boston: Allyn and Bacon, Inc. 1958.

Carlson, Richard O., *et al.,* eds., *Change Processes in the Public Schools.* Eugene, Oregon: Center for Advanced Study of Educational Administration, University of Oregon, 1965.

Culbertson, Jack, and Stephen P. Hencley, eds., *Preparing Administrators: New Perspectives.* Columbus, Ohio: University Council for Educational Administration, 1962.

Downey, Lawrence W., and Frederick Enns, eds., *The Social Sciences and Educational Administration.* Edmonton, Alberta, Canada: Division of Educational Administration, University of Alberta, 1963.

Griffiths, Daniel E., ed., *Behavioral Science and Educational Administration,* 63rd Yearbook of the National Society for the Study of Education. Chicago: The University of Chicago Press, 1964.

Griffiths, Daniel E., *Administrative Theory.* New York: Appleton-Century-Crofts, 1959.

Gross, Neal, and Robert E. Herriott, *The Professional Leadership of Elementary School Principals.* Washington, D.C.: The Cooperative Research Branch, Project No. 853, U.S. Office of Education, April 1964.

Gross, Neal, and Anne E. Trask, *Men and Women as Elementary School Principals.* Washington, D.C.: The Cooperative Research Branch, Project No. 853, U.S. Office of Education, June 1964.

Halpin, Andrew W., ed., *Administrative Theory in Education.* Chicago: Midwest Administration Center, The University of Chicago, 1958.

Halpin, Andrew W., and Don Croft, *The Organizational Climate of Schools.* Chicago: Midwest Administration Center, University of Chicago, 1963.

Hemphill, John K., Daniel E. Griffiths, and Norman N. Frederiksen, *Administrative Performance and Personality.* New York: Bureau of Publications, Teachers' College, Columbia University, 1962.

Jacobson, P. B., W. C. Reavis, and J. D. Logsdon, *The Effective School Principal* (2nd edition). Englewood Cliffs, N.J.: Prentice-Hall Inc., 1963.

Leu, Donald J., and Herbert C. Rudman, eds., *Preparation Programs for School Administrators: Common and Specialized Learnings*. East Lansing, Michigan: College of Education, Michigan State University, 1963.

McCleary, Lloyd E., and Stephen P. Hencley, *Secondary School Administration: Theoretical Bases of Professional Practice*. New York: Dodd, Mead and Co., 1965.

Otto, Henry J., and David C. Sanders, *Elementary School Organization and Administration* (4th edition). New York: Appleton-Century-Crofts, 1964.

Pierce, Paul Revere, *The Origin and Development of the Public School Principalship*. Chicago: The University of Chicago Press, 1935.

Tyler, Ralph W., and Virgil E. Herrick, eds., *Toward Improved Curriculum Theory*. Chicago: The University of Chicago Press, 1950.

Index

Index